Your Guide to the Orchestra
Through SOUNDS AND STORIES

Those Amazing Musical Instruments!

Genevieve Helsby

with Marin Alsop as Your Guide

SOURCEBOOKS
Jabberwocky
AN IMPRINT OF SOURCEBOOKS

Published by Sourcebooks Jabberwocky, an imprint of Sourcebooks, Inc.
P.O. Box 4410, Naperville, Illinois 60567-4410
(630) 961-3900
Fax: (630) 961-2168
www.sourcebooks.com

Originally published in the UK by Naxos Books, an imprint of Naxos Rights International Ltd.
Design and Layout (Naxos): Hannah Davies, Fruition - Creative Concepts
Design and Layout (Sourcebooks): Katie Olsen
CD-ROM design: Arthur Ka Wai Jenkins

Library of Congress Cataloging-in-Publication Data

Helsby, Genevieve.
  Those amazing musical instruments / by Genevieve Helsby with Marin
Alsop as your guide.
      p. cm.
  1. Musical instruments--Juvenile literature. I. Alsop, Marin. II.
Title.

ML460.H44 2007
784.19--dc22

                    2007013821

Printed and bound in China.
OGP 10 9 8 7 6 5 4 3 2

Source of Production: Prosperous Printing Factory, Shen Zhen, GuangDong Province, China
Date of production: 10/9/2009
Run Number: 11132

Those Amazing Musical Instruments!

by Genevieve Helsby

with **Marin Alsop**
as Your Guide

Marin Alsop in the Spotlight

Our guiding star describes what it's like to be in charge of the instruments...

Throughout this book you're going to see many different musical instruments. They may be played alone or in small groups of two, three, four or more. These are called duets, trios, quartets, and so on, depending on the number of players that are in the group. Taken all together, the instruments in this book comprise an orchestra – many musicians playing together.

Hearing an orchestra is easily one of the most thrilling experiences in life. I remember the very first time that I played in an orchestra and the amazing feelings I had. I sat way back in the second violins because I was quite new at playing and not very good yet. But I was still overcome by the enormity of the orchestra and the excitement of being a part of something so big. Being surrounded by sound – loud, pounding sounds and quiet, calming, beautiful sounds – that were created by so many kids working intensely together as a team was an inspiration. I felt transported to another place. I loved both the sounds and the teamwork.

The orchestra is certainly the biggest team you will ever experience: there are nearly 100 players on this team and NO ONE sits on the bench! Everyone is critical to the creation and success of the concert. There are players who must step out and take risks, like the woodwind and brass solo players, or the cymbal player. (You can imagine what would happen if the cymbal player made a mistake!) And there are players who remain slightly in the background but contribute just as much to the team's success, like the members of the string family.

When I first heard a big orchestra perform in concert I realized that I absolutely HAD to be a part of that experience. And since I was always quite bossy and a bit of a know-it-all, I decided right then and there that I would have to be in charge of the team! That was the moment that I decided to become a conductor.

Being a conductor is very much like being the captain of a team. The team members look toward you as a source of strength, encouragement and guidance. As the captain of the largest team around, the orchestra, I have a big responsibility to my players. I must give them positive feedback and bring out the best in each individual, while always remembering the good of the whole team.

Can you imagine being captain of a football team that has 100 members? It's a lot of work, but very rewarding! When I step up onto the podium and turn to face my orchestra, I see a disciplined, enthusiastic team ready for action. There are four distinct groups, or families, that form the team: strings, woodwinds, brass and percussion, and each family has its own leader.

Since the strings are the largest family in the orchestra, their leader, the first violinist, has

an extremely important role in relation to all of the families of instruments. This person is very much like the grandparent to all the families, or the elder statesperson, and has a special title in the orchestra, which is Concertmaster. The Concertmaster will walk on stage for a special bow at the start of every concert and will organize and oversee the tuning of the orchestra before the conductor enters. The Concertmaster is also responsible for coordinating the bowings of the string section, so that everyone is

bowing in the same direction at all times. That means that the Concertmaster must be in charge of 60 string players at all times. Can you imagine if their bowings were NOT uniform? It would be very distracting to watch 60 bows going this way and that with no plan at all!

I must admit I'm especially keen on the string family, because when I was growing up that was what I heard around the house. My father plays the violin; my mother plays the cello; and I play the violin. I can't imagine what it sounded like to our neighbors with all of us practicing away at once - our dog used to try to get in on the act, too, by singing along. What a racket that must have been! And there were only three (four counting the dog) of us. Just imagine what pandemonium could break loose with 60 people going at it all at once: that's why it's so important to have one person in charge of the entire string family.

The leader of the woodwind family is the oboe. The oboist sits right in the center of the woodwind family and gives the tuning note for the entire orchestra. This is a huge responsibility - and the first thing the audience hears - so the oboe usually feels very important.

The woodwind family contains four groups: oboes, flutes, clarinets and bassoons. What I like best about the woodwinds is that each group has an amazingly different and distinctive sound from the rest. Each musician must be an accomplished solo player to belong to the woodwind family and will often need to be able to play more than one kind of instrument. For example, the flutes can range from the lowest, the bass flute, all the way up to the absolute highest, the piccolo. So each group in the woodwind family has

many possible instruments. All of them, except the flutes, create their sounds by using what are called reeds. Often the oboists and the bassoonists make their own reeds, which is very challenging and time consuming. Of everyone in the orchestra, I think the woodwinds are the busiest.

The brass family is usually made up of four horns, three trumpets, three trombones and one tuba. They are the real muscle of the orchestra and can create enormous walls of sound one minute and beautiful, delicate melodies the next. I especially love the sound of the horns (they're called French horns but are NOT French). The horns are the real link between the woodwinds and the brass and can be both extremely soloistic, like the woodwinds, and then very forceful, like the rest of the brass.

I've noticed that the brass players often organize ball games and parties, which leads me to think that they have the most time on their hands! The truth is that the muscles used to produce sound, the face muscles, tire very quickly so if you play a brass instrument you can't practice as long as string players. Some people would say that's a good thing!

The last major family in the orchestra is the noisiest: the percussion family. This family adopts all the instruments that don't fit in anywhere else, so we find some unexpected instruments in there. For example, the percussion family includes the piano and the harp as well as whistles, xylophones and other strange instruments. The percussion family is the newest family in the orchestra and is still changing and growing. Composers seem to like looking around and adding in weird and wonderful things. I recently did a new piece that called for several wok tops and a whole range of flower pots. So I am now wary of composers who like to cook or garden. Oh, and brakedrums from cars are now standard percussion instruments, so watch out for those car buffs, too!

The orchestra never ceases to thrill and amaze me. The incredible variety and diversity of the four families of instruments and the way they complement each other and work together to produce powerful and profound sounds is endlessly exciting.

Which family would you like to join? It's up to you and I hope to see you as a member of the biggest team in the world: the orchestra.

To find out more about Marin Alsop, insert the CD-ROM and click on the Marin Alsop page.

About the Author

After gaining a distinction for piano performance at Durham University, **Genevieve Helsby** graduated with an MA in music and went on to spend three years as Literary Editor at Chandos Records. She then enjoyed a brief spell at Oxford University Press before taking up the post of Editorial Manager within Naxos, handling all books and educational titles. She is the author of *The Story of Classical Music* interactive CD-ROM, published by Naxos AudioBooks in 2004 and widely commended.

Author's Acknowledgments

Without Klaus Heymann, owner and founder of Naxos, this book would not have come about. His commitment to education is exceptional, and I have thoroughly enjoyed contributing to it in this way.

I would also like to thank several people for their unstinting support during the realization of this project, not least my family and friends. In particular, I am extremely grateful to Hannah Davies, whose tireless and talented design work, despite a punishing schedule from the author-cum-publisher, has been pivotal to this project's success. She may even be seen within the pages of this book, playing her own oboe and cor anglais! Arthur Ka Wai Jenkins has played a similarly indispensable, round-the-clock role, not only in designing the CD-ROM but also as photographer and recording engineer. Finally, I owe a huge debt to Nicolas Soames for his belief in my capacity as author, his constant support and encouragement, and his making it all possible.

Many other people have made vital contributions. Naxos Books and I would like to thank the following for their valuable advice and/or assistance with pictures:

The Royal College of Music Junior Department

Junior Department

Photographs and names of all who were involved in the recording and photography session on 14.5.05, as well as biographical details of the department, may be found on the CD-ROM.

www.yamaha-music.co.uk

Yamaha, Selmer, Vincent Bach, Hill & Co. - Welwyn, Arthur Ka Wai Jenkins, Alasdair Malloy, Rolf Tinlin, Peter Newble, Karen Aplin, Andrew Lang, Joe Berry, Ralf Ehlers, Grammenos Chalkias, Rebecca Helsby, Paul Archibald, Colin Lawson, Adrian France, Alex Heffes, Maya Magub, Sarah Butcher, Claire Wadsworth, Rachel Walters

Compatible
Mac. If the C
automaticall
page 9 fo

About the CD-ROM

On the enclosed CD-ROM, you can listen to samples of each instrument, as well as learn more about the musical families, their history, and some "star players" — real-life musicians.

Insert the CD-ROM into your computer and it will automatically start*.
Click "enter" to view the main menu:

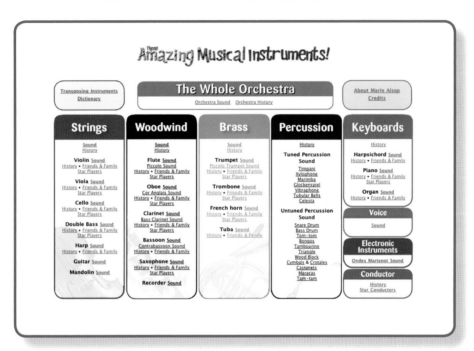

Under each main "family" category, you can click on <u>Sound</u> to hear examples of each instrument featured in a piece with other instruments, or playing its highest and lowest note by itself. Each category also includes links to more information.

Throughout the book, when you see this icon, you can launch the CD-ROM and follow links that relate to the page you're reading.

*If the CD-ROM does not automatically start:

In Windows: Go to My Computer. Select the CD-ROM (usually the "D" drive), and click "File," then "Open" to view the contents of the CD-ROM. Select the file "Index.htm" and click "File," then "Open" to start.

In Mac: The CD-ROM should appear on your desktop. Select the CD-ROM, and click "File," then "Open" to view the contents of the CD-ROM. Select the file "Index.htm" and click "File," then "Open" to start.

This CD-ROM requires a CD-ROM drive, web browser, and sound.

If you are having difficulty with the CD-ROM, please email **instruments@ sourcebooks.com** for assistance.

CONTENTS

Musical Instrument Families

Instruments are grouped into "families." Like any other family,
an instrument family has members with certain things in common.
People in a human family sometimes look or sound similar;
it's the same with instruments.

When these four musical families come together, they become an orchestra:

Strings

all have strings

Violin
Viola
Cello
Double bass

Woodwind

all originally
made of wood

Flute
Oboe
Clarinet
Bassoon

Brass

all usually
made of brass

Trumpet
Trombone
French horn
Tuba

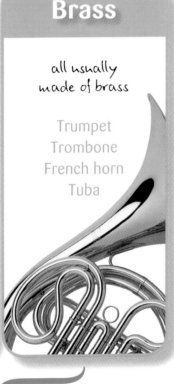

Percussion

all are struck
or shaken to make
a sound [ouch!]

Tuned percussion
instruments produce
exact pitches

Untuned percussion
instruments produce
irregular pitches

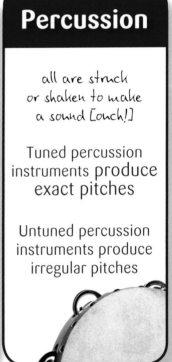

Wind

all are tubes for blowing down
(that creates the 'wind')

But these families have some odd relatives.
Did you know that there's a "heckelphone"?
What about an "ophicleide"?!

There are even strange, electronic instruments.
Have you heard of an "ondes martenot" before?
Or a "theremin"? In the next few pages, all will be
revealed.

What *is* an orchestra?

An orchestra is a fantastic fusion of musical sounds! The orchestra itself is one giant instrument. The conductor "plays" this instrument, controlling it, molding it, guiding it, making it louder, softer, faster, slower.

The orchestra performs music written by a composer. This music is like an enormous jigsaw puzzle: every musician's part is like a piece of the puzzle, fitting perfectly with all the rest to create a picture in sound.

When we just say "orchestra," we mean the big symphony orchestra that grew up in Europe over 250 years ago.

The word "symphony" means sounds that go together well. And in the 18th century, composers started writing pieces called "symphonies" for the orchestra to play.

CD-ROM ▶

Hear the instruments! Click "Orchestra Sound" to hear examples of the whole orchestra playing together.

Seating Plan

When the orchestra comes together, the families each have a particular place to sit. It's very organized! Can you imagine the chaos if it weren't?

Here is a common seating plan for the orchestra:

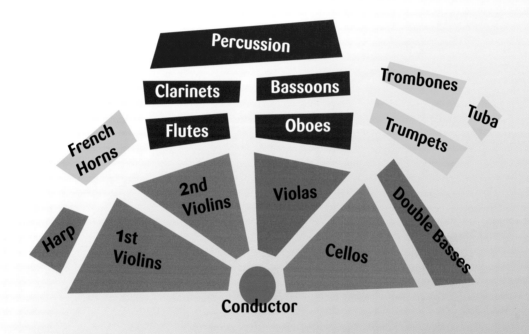

Orchestras around the world

Gamelan orchestras in Indonesia are full of exotic percussion instruments.

Gagaku orchestras in Japan play slow, majestic music for royal courts.

There are even Peruvian pan-pipe orchestras, Chinese drum and gong orchestras, African drumming groups, Vietnamese court orchestras, Jewish klezmer bands, Scandinavian wind orchestras, African Pygmy horn ensembles… orchestras are everywhere!

Closer to home, there are symphony orchestras (the biggest kind), chamber orchestras (smaller ones) and string orchestras (just string instruments).

Sound

Different musical instruments make a whole variety of noises. But they all have one basic thing in common: they produce sound.

Vibration

Sound is all about vibration (something moving). If you strike a saucepan lid, the noise you hear is made by the saucepan lid vibrating. If you blow on a blade of grass, that squeaky sound you get is because you've made the grass vibrate.

So, if you bow or pluck the strings of a violin, they vibrate and that produces a sound. If you blow down an oboe, the air vibrates down its tube and that produces a sound.

The sounds are different because of the instrument's body. It's like your own voice: it doesn't match anyone else's because each person's body is slightly different.

The faster the vibration, the higher the sound.

The slower the vibration, the lower the sound.

Sound Waves

These vibrations create what are called "sound waves." Scientists can actually measure these sound waves and show them as a picture. Each instrument produces a particular kind of sound, so the shapes of the waves are all a bit different:

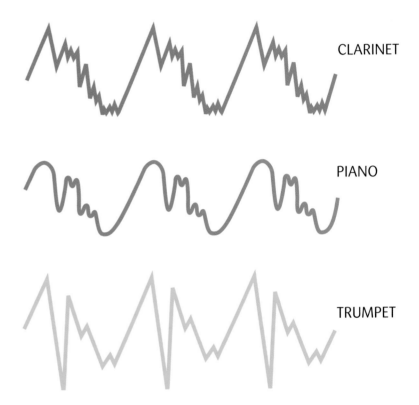

CLARINET

PIANO

TRUMPET

Remember, remember

If a string is **long**,
the sound is **low**.

If a string is **short**,
the sound is **high**.

If a tube is **long**,
the sound is **low**.

If a tube is **short**,
the sound is **high**.

Size

Small instruments are higher-pitched (have higher sounds) and big instruments are lower-pitched (have lower sounds). This is because of the instrument's body.

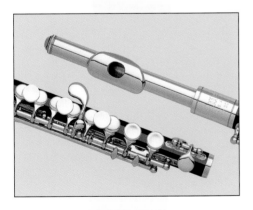

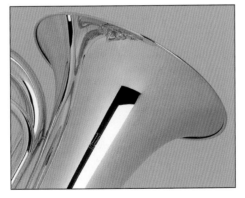

The vibration that you've created by blowing, plucking, striking etc. resonates somewhere before it comes out as a sound. This lets the sound grow and develop. Higher sounds don't need so much room to develop, and the instruments are small (like the piccolo). Lower sounds need a lot of room to develop, and the instruments are large (like the enormous tuba, the double bass, or the bass drum).

THE STRINGS

Harp

Double Bass

String instruments have always been beautiful - to see and to hear. They have a stylish, elegant shape. Good violins aren't built by machines like identical cars in a factory: each one is crafted by hand out of top-quality wood and carefully varnished. Old instruments were sometimes even decorated with beautiful patterns.

Cello   **Viola**   **Violin**

Long Ago

Nobody is sure when the first string instruments appeared. In cave paintings thousands of years old, it looks as though hunters may have discovered that their bows and arrows could do more than kill animals. A hunter might have plucked the string of his hunting bow for amusement. Then perhaps he discovered that if he made the string shorter, the note was higher; and if he drew another bow across the original bow, it produced a noise. What an exciting discovery!

Did you know?

Sometimes, when a player attacks the strings for loud, dramatic music, the bow starts losing hair! Sometimes you see one dangling from a player's bow in the middle of a concert before he or she yanks it off completely. It doesn't really matter: there are plenty more hairs, so you don't hear the difference. A bow would never go bald in just one concert!

Today

There are two distinct groups of string instruments:

1) **Bowed:** You draw a bow across the strings (violin, viola, cello, double bass).

2) **Plucked:** You pluck the strings with your fingers (harp, guitar) or a little piece of plastic called a pick (guitar, mandolin). The violin, viola, cello and double bass can also be plucked.

A harpist plucking the strings

The shorter & thinner the string, the higher the note.

The longer & thicker the string, the lower the note.

All have these basic things in common:

- There are strings made of a material that will produce a sound.
- The strings are activated by something (fingers, a pick or a bow).
- A hollow box is put under the strings to make the sound louder.
- The length and tension of the strings affects how high or low the notes are. ("Tension" is how tight or slack they are.)

On all instruments except the harp, the player's fingers "stop" the strings. This means that the fingers press down at different points on the strings to alter the length used for playing: when the strings are then bowed or plucked, different notes are produced.

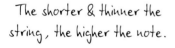

The Violin Family

The violin, viola, cello and double bass are full-time members of the orchestra. They are known as the "violin family," since they all look quite similar.

Bodily features

Arched "belly" and back.

Gently curved shoulders (except for the double bass).

Holes in an "f" shape for the sound to come out of.

Carved scroll above the peg box.

Makers

Italy was the center of violin making in the 1600s: whole families became famous for it. They crafted their instruments using the finest materials they could find in their quest for the most beautiful sound. The Amati and Guarneri families were the talk of Cremona, along with Antonio Stradivari and his family.

The end of the bow where you hold it, is called the "frog"!

Stradivari

Mr Stradivari lived to 90 and made over 1,000 top-quality violins, violas and cellos. Today, his instruments are still the most desirable of all.

The amazing thing about these high-class string instruments is that, unlike most things, they get better as they get older! They're worth more and more money as time goes on.

These days, a "Stradivarius" violin could cost about $1.5 million!

Construction of the Instruments

Body: Made of varnished wood in an elegant "S" shape.
Maple for the back.
Spruce for the front and the rest of the body.
Ebony and rosewood for the fingerboard and pegs.

Strings: Years ago the strings were made of sheep gut [yuck!]; these days they're normally made of steel or nylon.

Bow: Horsehair attached to a stick of pernambuco wood. The horsehair is rubbed with sticky stuff called "rosin" made from tree sap.

Each string is stretched vertically from the tailpiece at the bottom, across a little wooden bridge – which lifts the string a bit – to the top, where it is wound around a peg.

Why are there **four strings**? There could just be one very long string and it would do the same job. But it would be so long, you'd break your arm trying to play it! So this long string is divided into four, which makes life much easier. It also means you can play two or three notes at once by drawing the bow across more than one string. This is called double- or triple-stopping.

Bows are important too. You might think that a bit of horsehair on a stick is pretty easy to make, but no! Good ones are expensive. They are light and flexible, and help to produce the best quality of sound.

BRIDGE

TAILPIECE

PEG

FINGERBOARD

Before beginning, the player has to make sure the instrument is "in tune" – i.e. that its strings are at the exact pitch they should be. This is done by twisting the pegs at the top to tighten or slacken them. The tighter they are, the sharper (higher in pitch) they will be; the slacker they are, the flatter (lower in pitch) they will be.

Scroll with tuning pegs

How is the sound made?

1) The bow is drawn across a string (or the string is plucked) with the right hand.
2) The string vibrates.
3) These vibrations travel through the bridge and into the whole body of the instrument before emerging as a rich sound.
4) The left hand presses (or "stops") the strings on the fingerboard for different notes.

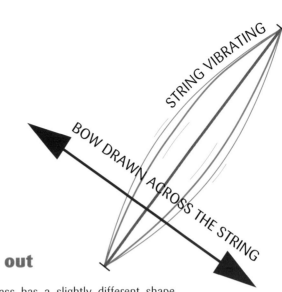

STRING VIBRATING

BOW DRAWN ACROSS THE STRING

Rubbing the bow with rosin is a bit like rubbing the tip of a pool cue with chalk: chalk prevents the cue from slipping on the ball; rosin prevents the bow from slipping on the strings. If the bow didn't grip the strings and make them vibrate, it would just slide across them and no sound would come out.

Odd one out

The double bass has a slightly different shape from that of the violin, viola and cello. Because of it's size, it is molded in a particular way to make it easier to play. Its shoulders, for example, are more sloped so that players can reach over them without injuring themselves!

Double bass

Cello

Viola

Violin

Lining them up...

The instruments get bigger... but their bows get shorter!

Violin bow

Viola bow

Cello bow

Double bass bow

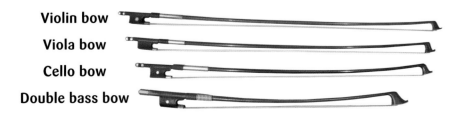

Occasionally, strings snap! It can be a bit of a shock when it happens. Players always carry spare strings, and know how to replace them.

Special Effects

String instruments have an incredible range of expression. That's why composers have always loved writing music for them. They can sing beautifully, shriek angrily or do any of the following clever things:

Pizzicato:	Plucking – this is used a lot.
Vibrato:	Used nearly all the time – the finger wobbles backwards and forwards very fast on the string to make the note sound richer and more attractive.
Double/triple-stopping:	Playing more than one note at a time, to make a chord.
Tremolo:	"Trembling" – the bow is shaken very quickly backwards and forwards on the string. The effect can be frightening or exciting.
Spiccato:	Short, bouncy strokes played at the middle of the bow.
Ricochet:	The bow is basically thrown at the string (but in a controlled way, without letting go!) so that it rebounds sharply.
Sul ponticello:	Playing very near the bridge, which gives a creepy but crisp sound.
Col legno:	The wooden stick of the bow is struck against the strings. The sound is quite harsh.
Muted:	A small piece of rubber – the "mute" – is placed on top of the bridge. It makes the sound quieter and more muffled: it can change the whole mood of a piece.
Glissando:	The fingers slide along the fingerboard while the note is played. It makes the sound swoop up (or down – depending which way the fingers slide).
Harmonics:	At specific places on the strings, the finger just touches lightly: when the bow is pulled across the string it makes a magical, hollow ringing sound.

Did you know

Q Are bows really made of horsehair?

A **Yes!** Horses in northern climates have stronger tail hair, so Siberian horses are great for bows. But hairs are taken from horses that are already dead, and the horses are not killed for it.

Strings in the Orchestra

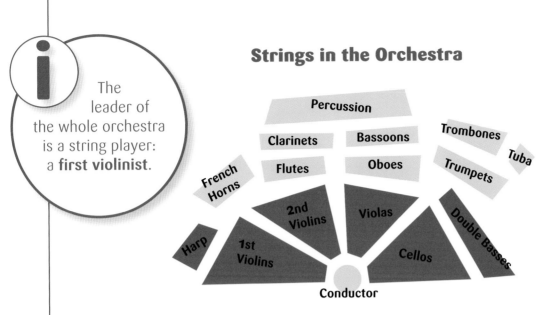

Members of the string family (shown above) form the heart of the orchestra: they surround the conductor and like to keep busy. Just as a body would be dead without a beating heart, an orchestra would be dead without a lively string section!

A typical orchestra today has:
16 first violins
14 second violins
12 violas
10 cellos
8 double basses

- but this varies a lot: it depends on the piece of music, the size of the concert platform, and the conductor's preference. Some orchestral pieces may include the harp, guitar, or mandolin.

Playing Together - Chamber Music

The string section of the orchestra (not including the harp) is unique: all the instruments are basically the same. They vary in size, so they range in sound - from very high to very low. But they blend perfectly together because they are all built in the same way and have the same sort of sound. So outside the symphony orchestra, there are many "chamber" pieces written just for them.

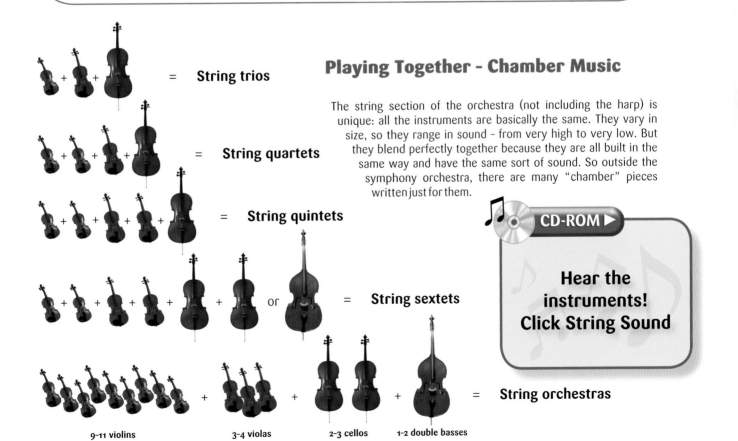

CD-ROM ▶

Hear the instruments! Click String Sound

The Violin
Leader of the Pack

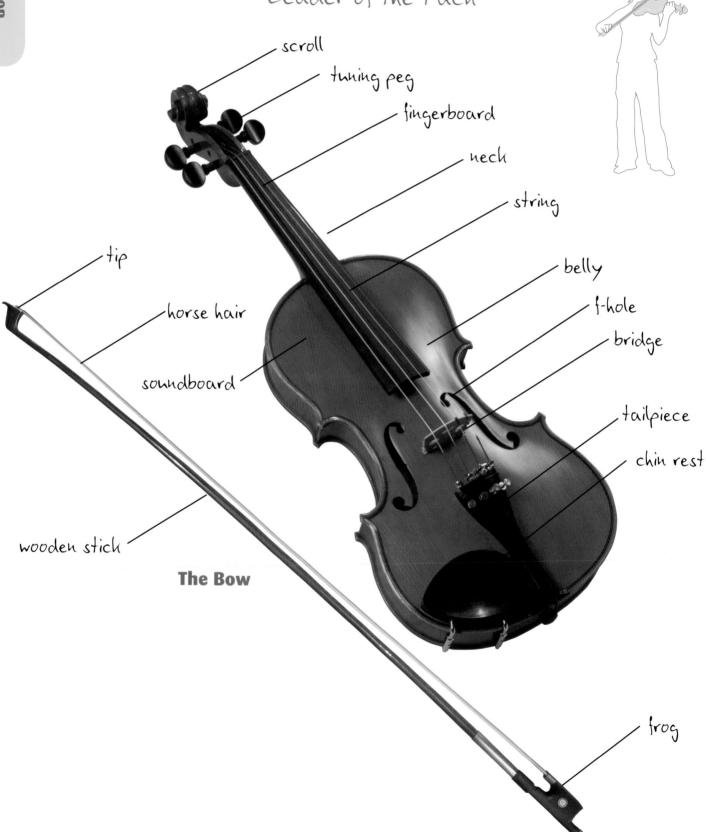

scroll

tuning peg

fingerboard

neck

string

belly

f-hole

bridge

tip

horse hair

soundboard

tailpiece

chin rest

wooden stick

The Bow

frog

Overall

The violin is a jack of all trades: singing, shouting, leaping around, whispering, whining, making sounds that are high and wispy, low and gutsy, warm and mellow, soft and silky, shrill and loud... it can do anything, and loves to be the center of attention!

It's the highest and most agile member of the string family. For over three centuries, many people have seen the violin as the most extraordinary and beautiful instrument ever invented.

It's at home in a whole variety of situations (solo music, orchestral music, chamber music, folk, pop, world, jazz) and takes up its role of concertmaster quite happily. From around 1600 to today, the violins have been at the heart of the orchestra.

The great physicist **Albert Einstein** was a good and enthusiastic violinist: he played chamber music and taught the instrument. But perhaps he wasn't that good: apparently, in a rehearsal of a Haydn string quartet, he failed for the fourth time to begin playing his part at the correct time. So the cellist looked up and said, "The problem with you, Albert, is that you simply can't count."

Nicolò Paganini was such an amazing wizard on the violin in the 19th century that people thought he was in league with the devil. They couldn't understand how he could play so spectacularly, using so many clever effects (pizzicato, harmonics etc.). He would even wow audiences with tricks, such as playing a really difficult piece on one string, having snapped off the other three on purpose!

Violins in the Orchestra

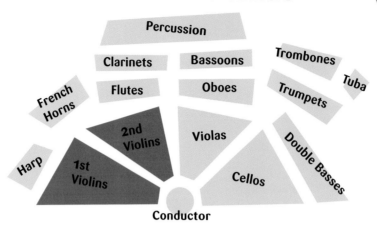

Percussion

Clarinets | Bassoons | Trombones | Tuba

French Horns | Flutes | Oboes | Trumpets

Harp | 2nd Violins | Violas | Double Basses

1st Violins | Cellos

Conductor

Today, top-quality violins by legendary makers such as Amati, Stradivari and Guarneri cost many thousands of dollars!

The violin section is the largest in the orchestra: there are often around 30. They're divided into first violins (playing the highest parts) and second violins (playing lower parts). The first violinist, called the concertmaster, leads the orchestra, and sits at the front. In a concert, the concertmaster comes on stage separately, just before the conductor, and gets a round of applause.

Did you know ?

In the 1780s a Frenchman called François Tourte made a brilliant bow which matched Stradivari's brilliant violins. His bow was thinner, longer and more flexible. It became the model for all others.

In some ways, you might think it's easiest to be a violinist: there are so many people around you playing the same thing that if you were to go wrong nobody would really notice. And if you couldn't play it, perhaps you could just pretend! **Right?**

Wrong! Miming on a violin isn't easy: the bow ends up touching the string and making sounds you weren't planning for. And although you don't stand out as much as the wind players, the challenge is for everyone to play perfectly together. As soon as one person is slightly off, the sound becomes messy and the orchestra immediately stops sounding professional.

Violins are given a lot of wonderful, soaring melodies: the visual effect of 30 bows rushing up and down at exactly the same time, producing a full and satisfying sound, is very dramatic. The concertmaster may also be given a solo: the clear, sweet sound of the violin can be heard right above the orchestra.

One of the most versatile instruments, the violin can be found in:

Concertos: In these, the spotlight is on one violinist at the front of the stage, with the orchestra playing behind.

Chamber music: Duets, trios, quartets, quintets, sextets etc. – sometimes for strings only, sometimes with other instruments. String quartets (for four people) are very important: the first violin plays the highest part, the second violin plays a bit lower, the viola plays a bit lower than that, and the cello plays at the bottom.

Jazz: The violin is sometimes found here. Stephane Grappelli was a famous French jazz violinist.

Pop music: Electric violins are sometimes used in pop music.

Solo pieces: No shortage of these, for violin and piano, or just violin.

World music: The violin is played in many other kinds of music, especially folk music, from Scotland ("folk fiddle") to Hungary ("gypsy" violin) to India.

Highs & Lows pitch range

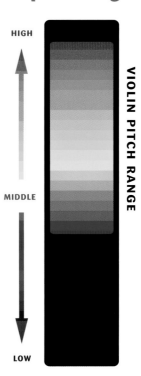

HIGH

MIDDLE

LOW

VIOLIN PITCH RANGE

How do you play it?

1) Take the top of the violin in your left hand.
2) Bring the instrument around so that the bottom sits underneath your chin.
3) With your right hand, draw the bow across the strings, or pluck them.

For more about the violin's construction, how the sound is made, and how to play, flick back to pages 22–24.

CD-ROM ▶

Hear the instruments! Click Violin Sound under "Strings"

Actor Russell Crowe learned the violin for his role in the blockbuster film *Master and Commander*. According to him, leaping around with a sword and shield among thousands of enemies was easy compared with learning the violin! This is what he said:

"You can take your helicopter stunts and your tiger fights and your mathematics - it's got nothing to do with how difficult an instrument the violin is."

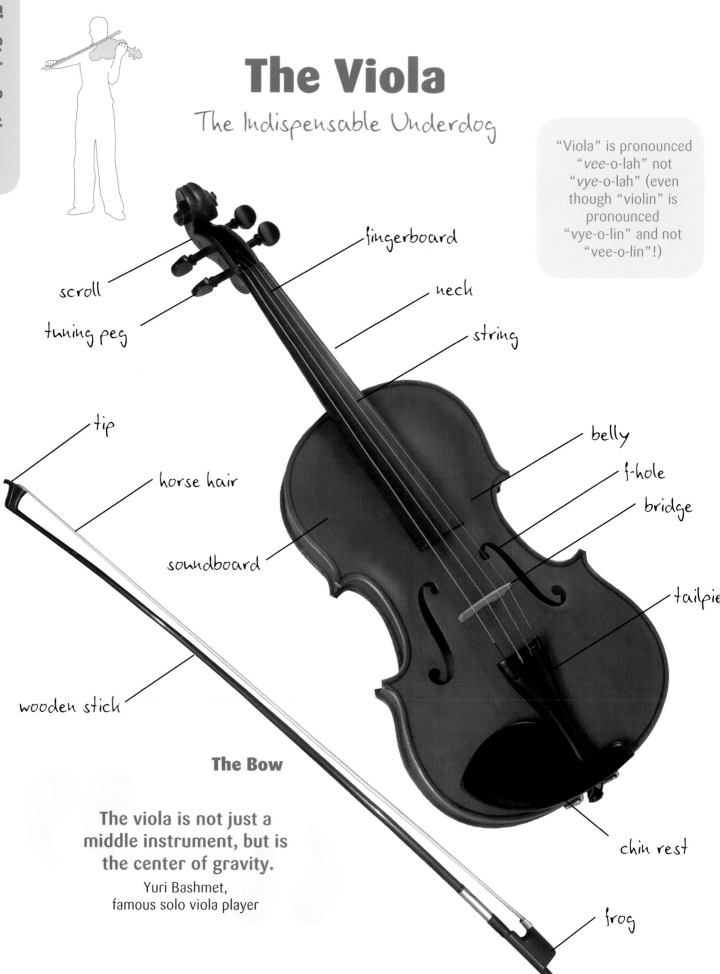

The Viola
The Indispensable Underdog

"Viola" is pronounced "*vee*-o-lah" not "*vye*-o-lah" (even though "violin" is pronounced "vye-o-lin" and not "vee-o-lin"!)

fingerboard

scroll

neck

tuning peg

string

tip

belly

horse hair

f-hole

bridge

soundboard

tailpie

wooden stick

The Bow

chin rest

The viola is not just a middle instrument, but is the center of gravity.
Yuri Bashmet,
famous solo viola player

frog

Overall

So, is the viola just "a big violin"? No! The poor viola has struggled with this label for years. Viola players hate it because it suggests that they're simply violinists with a clumsy, oversized instrument stuck under their chin.

In fact, the viola *looks* like a big violin and you play it in the exactly the same way. Many violinists, even famous ones, have had a stab at performing on it. But in the end, it needs an expert. It's a deep and soulful instrument which produces a very different character of sound from that of the violin.

Viola v. Violin

Size: The viola is bigger than a violin. The exact size has never been agreed on, so each viola varies a tiny bit.

The wood is the same thickness as the violin's wood, so it's a thinner instrument for its size.

The strings are longer and a bit thicker, so they sound darker and less delicate than a violin's.

The bow of the viola is shorter and heavier.

Longer strings and a **larger fingerboard** mean big stretches for the fingers.

Because the viola's register (the range of notes it can play) is in between those of the violin and cello, viola music is written using a **special clef** called the "alto clef." It makes sure the notes are easy to read and don't fall off the staff.

If the notes for the viola were written in the treble clef, like they are for the violin, a lot of them would be reaching down from the bottom, like this:

If they were written in the bass clef, like they are for the cello, a lot of them would be climbing up on extra little lines, like this:

So, to make things easier to read, you get this:

Challenge

The viola has never become a popular *solo* instrument, despite having a few star players. Its sound isn't as bright as a violin's or as rich as a cello's. So, when the spotlight's shining and the pressure's on, it's a challenge to stop it from sounding like a violin with a frog in its throat.

Violas in the Orchestra

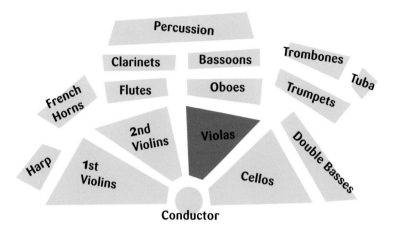

Percussion

Clarinets Bassoons Trombones Tuba

French Horns Flutes Oboes Trumpets

2nd Violins Violas Double Basses

Harp 1st Violins Cellos

Conductor

Violas are middle-men: they fill in the notes between the higher violins and the lower cellos. The orchestra needs them, but you'd need really good ears to pick out the violas when all the strings are playing.

There are usually 12 violas in a symphony orchestra. They sit right in front of the conductor, in between the violins and cellos.

Mozart, Haydn and two other composers used to spend many evenings playing string quartets together. For these, Mozart always played the viola part: he liked to be right in the middle of the music.

Viola d'amore

The viola d'amore (meaning "viola of love") is different from the regular viola. It's an early instrument that was popular in the 17th and 18th centuries. Belonging to the viol family, it has sloping shoulders, like the double bass, and more strings than a modern viola. But it's still held under the chin. In the 20th century, it became popular again and has had pieces written specifically for it.

Apart from the orchestra, you can also find violas in:

Concertos: Just a few good ones. The viola is not such an obvious soloist as the high, soaring violin or the rich, sonorous cello.

Chamber music: Many string quartets - the viola plays between the two violins and the cello. Other chamber pieces, often with strings and piano, sometimes with a woodwind instrument like the clarinet.

Solo pieces: Some, but fewer than for violin or cello.

How do you play it?

Just like a violin! Except that the fingers are stretched out further to reach the notes.

For more about the viola's construction, how the sound is made, and how to play, flick back to pages 22-24.

i Only 10 violas made by the famous Stradivari survive today, compared with about 50 cellos and over 500 violins.

Highs & Lows pitch range

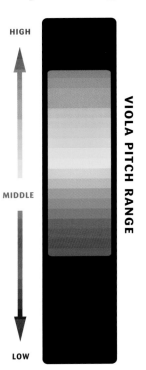

HIGH

MIDDLE

LOW

VIOLA PITCH RANGE

Hector Berlioz wrote *Harold in Italy* - a kind of viola concerto - for Paganini, but Paganini refused to play it! Being the biggest show-off the world had ever known on the violin, he thought the viola part in Berlioz's piece wasn't flashy enough. When he finally heard it performed, he realized how silly he'd been and what a great piece it was.

CD-ROM ▶

Hear the instruments! Click Viola Sound under "Strings"

The Violoncello
("Cello")
Rich Uncle of the String Family

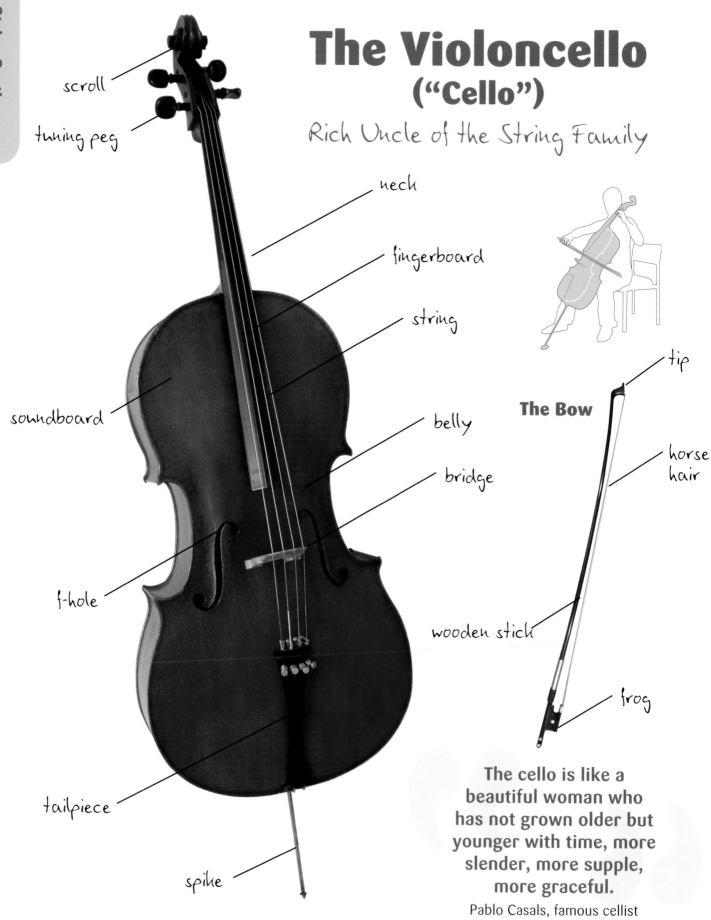

scroll

tuning peg

neck

fingerboard

string

soundboard

belly

bridge

f-hole

tailpiece

spike

The Bow

tip

horse hair

wooden stick

frog

The cello is like a beautiful woman who has not grown older but younger with time, more slender, more supple, more graceful.

Pablo Casals, famous cellist

Overall

The cello can sing like a human being. It sounds warm and deep, and communicates feelings and emotions just like a singer does. Bigger than the violin and viola but smaller than the double bass, it sits in the orchestra with authority. Cellists generally don't compete with each other (which the violinists sometimes do) but simply enjoy playing together.

Cellos in the Orchestra

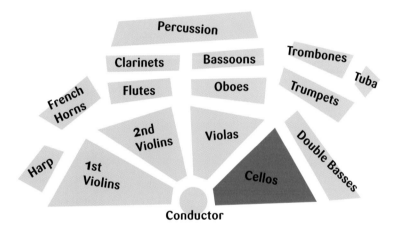

An orchestra normally has about 10 cellos. Being low-pitched, they often provide a necessary bass line in the music. But sometimes they get great passionate melodies to enjoy, which sweep magnificently through the rest of the orchestra.

It's a fact...

The cello developed in the 1500s with the violin, as part of the "violin family." So all the famous Italian violin makers (like Amati and Stradivari) made cellos too.

Sometimes the cellos swap places with the second violins, so that they sit between the first violins and violas. This can give an interesting stereo effect. But in that position, the second violins end up being angled away from the audience: their sound holes point the wrong way and people can't hear them very well. So normally, the cellos sit at the front, opposite the first violins and to the right of the conductor – as above.

Cellos also play in:

Concertos: Many of these have been written for the cello – its heart-rending sound in particular has attracted composers to write for it.

Chamber music: Plenty with just string instruments, and other pieces with strings, piano and woodwind instruments.

Solo pieces: Again, many – with and without piano accompaniment. J.S. Bach wrote six famous unaccompanied cello suites.

How do you play it?

The cello is an even bigger violin than the viola, but stick this one under your chin and you'd probably break your arm - not to mention stabbing your neck with its spike!

Instead:
1) The cellist sits down.
2) The cello is placed between the knees of the cellist.
3) The spike is used to anchor the cello at the necessary angle, so that it doesn't slide all over the floor.
4) Holding the "neck" in the left hand, the cellist draws the bow across the strings, or plucks them, with the right hand.

Sometimes, a really enthusiastic cellist will rock around on the chair while playing, body and cello swaying together with the music! It's a satisfying instrument to hear, to feel and to play.

For more about the cello's construction, how the sound is made, and how to play, flick back to pages 22-24.

Highs & Lows pitch range

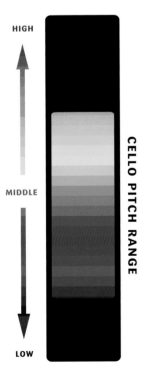

HIGH

MIDDLE

LOW

CELLO PITCH RANGE

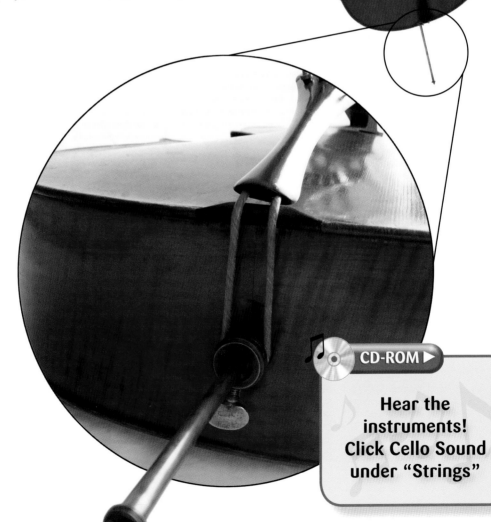

CD-ROM ▶

Hear the instruments! Click Cello Sound under "Strings"

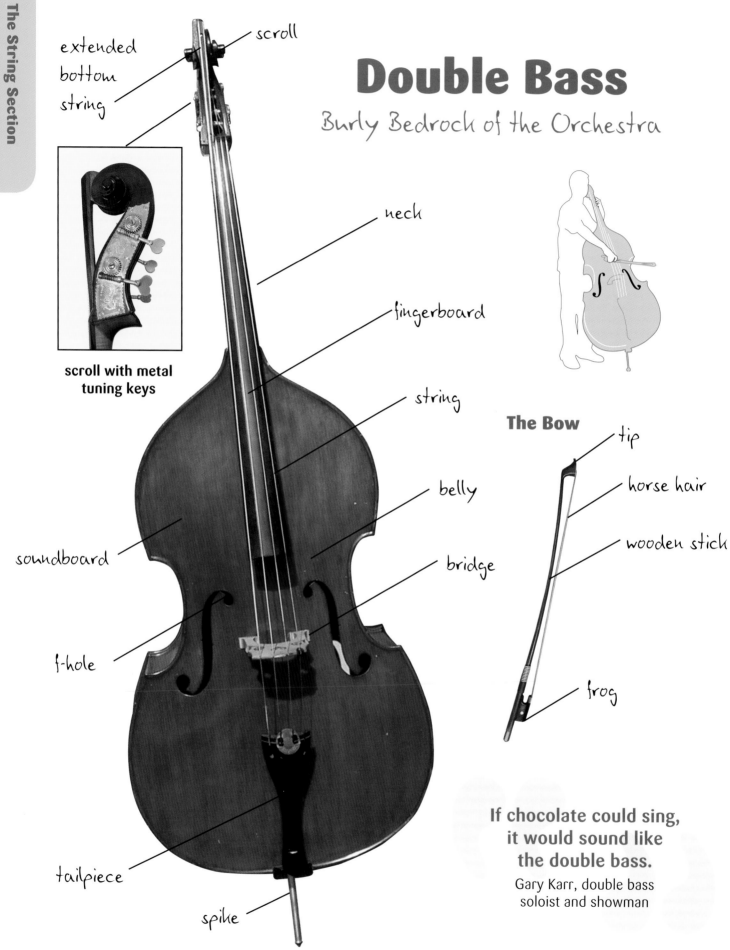

extended
bottom
string

scroll

Double Bass
Burly Bedrock of the Orchestra

neck

fingerboard

scroll with metal
tuning keys

string

The Bow

tip

belly

horse hair

soundboard

wooden stick

bridge

f-hole

frog

tailpiece

**If chocolate could sing,
it would sound like
the double bass.**

Gary Karr, double bass
soloist and showman

spike

Overall

The double bass is enormous! This giant of the string section would definitely not fit under your chin or between your knees. If you tried either, you'd probably be in pain for a long time afterwards... The bass is taller than a person and wider than a wheelbarrow. It's amazing that anyone chooses to drag it around to rehearsals and concerts, only to be stuck on the outskirts of the orchestra playing all the bottom notes.

But bass players are happy doing what they do! They are at the edge of the orchestra - but they perch on high stools and can look over the top of everyone else. And the instrument isn't quite as heavy as you'd think. Don't forget that the wooden body is hollow. Inside, it's all air.

i The double basses are sometimes called "the wardrobes" - because they line up like tall wardrobes along the edge of the orchestra!

Double Basses in the Orchestra

The name "double bass" is often shortened to just "**bass**."

Percussion

Clarinets   Bassoons   Trombones

French Horns   Flutes   Oboes   Trumpets   Tuba

2nd Violins   Violas   Double Basses

Harp   1st Violins   Cellos

Conductor

Pretty tunes are all very well, but they need support. There are normally eight double basses in a symphony orchestra, and they give solid support beneath everyone else's ups and downs. They do have tunes to play sometimes, but not very often.

The powerful low notes are fantastic: they can make the hairs on the back of your neck stand on end. If you're very near the instrument, you can even feel the vibration.

Double basses can also bring a piece of music to life, dancing rhythmically underneath the higher melodies.

Did you know

In the 18th century there was a composer called **Carl Ditters von Dittersdorf**. Today, he's remembered for his good double bass music *and* his funny name.

> To go up or down just one note on the double bass means nearly a complete hand-span on the fingerboard. Can you imagine playing a scale? It's not easy!

Concertos and Solo pieces: Historically there haven't been many solos written for double basses, but the number is increasing gradually.

Chamber music: Little compared to the rest of the violin family. But Schubert's "Trout" Quintet is a famous example – one of the happiest pieces of music ever written!

Jazz and Rock music: Particularly in jazz, where bouncy bass lines liven up many recordings. The player stands up and plays pizzicato (plucks the strings). Both styles give the double bass the chance to shed its classical image.

The double bass has an early ancestor called the viol. It gave the double bass features that the other violin family instruments don't have, like sloping shoulders, and sometimes a flat back. But the rest of the double bass – such as its f-holes, the wood and the way you play it – fits into the violin family.

Did you know ?

Some basses have five strings, and some have four with an extension for the bottom notes (see main picture on page 38).

The double bass has a pretty cool life outside the orchestra: it loves jazz! Its strings ping energetically like little musical drums, underneath other instruments like the piano and the saxophone.

A viol

How do you play it?

1) Perch on a high stool, behind the instrument.
2) Hold the neck with your left hand.
3) Lean over the double bass to draw the bow across the strings, or pluck them with your right hand.

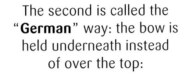

Hear the instruments! Click Double Bass Sound under "Strings"

Bow Holds

There are two ways of holding the bow.

The first is called the "**French**" way, and this is like the rest of the violin family:

The second is called the "**German**" way: the bow is held underneath instead of over the top:

But the way the bow makes the string vibrate is exactly the same as on the violin.

For more about the double bass's construction, how the sound is made, and how to play, flick back to pages 22-24.

Family Highs & Lows - Pitch Ranges Together

HIGH

MIDDLE

LOW

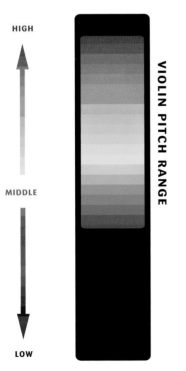

VIOLIN PITCH RANGE

VIOLA PITCH RANGE

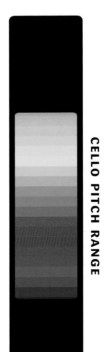

CELLO PITCH RANGE

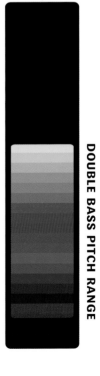

DOUBLE BASS PITCH RANGE

The Harp
Heavenly Guest of Honor

tuning pin

neck

string (47 of these, a mixture of nylon, gut, and metal)

Harp strings have different colors depending on their note: All "C" strings are red, and all "F" strings are black. This helps the harpist find them quickly.

pillar or column

soundboard

wooden frame

pedal

feet

The harp is special. It has a delicate, angelic sound, as if it has come from another world. For this reason, it's been linked with heaven - in music, paintings and books.

Overall

Many old harps were decorated with beautiful carvings.

The harp is in a world of its own. It's a string instrument, but it's completely different from the violin, viola, cello and double bass. It looks different, it's played differently, and its history is unconnected with those instruments.

It's thousands of years old. There were harps in Ancient Egypt: we know this because they feature in cave paintings. It spread across the world, and many countries and cultures made their own versions of the same instrument.

The concert harp (the type used in orchestras and pictured on the opposite page) has a triangular wooden frame with strings stretched from top to bottom and pedals on the base.

Harps in the Orchestra

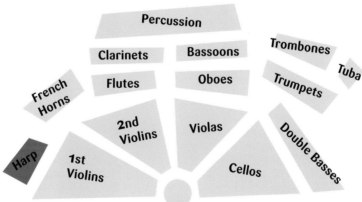

You won't always see harps in the orchestra, because not every piece needs them. When they are there, their unusual, silvery sound comes floating through with a kind of magical effect.

There might be just one harp, perhaps two. When Wagner wrote for six of them in his *Ring* cycle (a gigantic work containing four operas and lasting for hours!) he was, as usual, asking for more than most composers. As for Berlioz, demanding 10 in his *Damnation of Faust*... that's just greedy!

Did you know?

The harp is sometimes used in wedding receptions, restaurants and hotels to create a kind of luxurious atmosphere for the guests.

You might find a harp in:

Folk music: The harp has always had a big role to play here - in Ireland, Wales and Scotland in particular.

Concertos: Not many, but a highlight is Mozart's Flute and Harp Concerto.

Chamber music: Again, not a lot - but Ravel's *Introduction and Allegro* for harp, flute, clarinet and string quartet is a shining example.

Solo pieces: Not enough! But more are being written all the time. Many well-known pieces for other instruments are also arranged for the harp to play.

How do you play it?

1) You sit on a stool and lean the harp towards you with the pillar furthest away.

2) You pluck the strings with both hands, using the left hand for the lower (bass) notes, and the right for the higher (treble) ones.

3) Your feet use the pedals to make notes sharper (higher) or flatter (lower).

Every single string has to be tuned by the player before a rehearsal or concert. So harpists have to arrive before everyone else to make sure their harp is in tune.

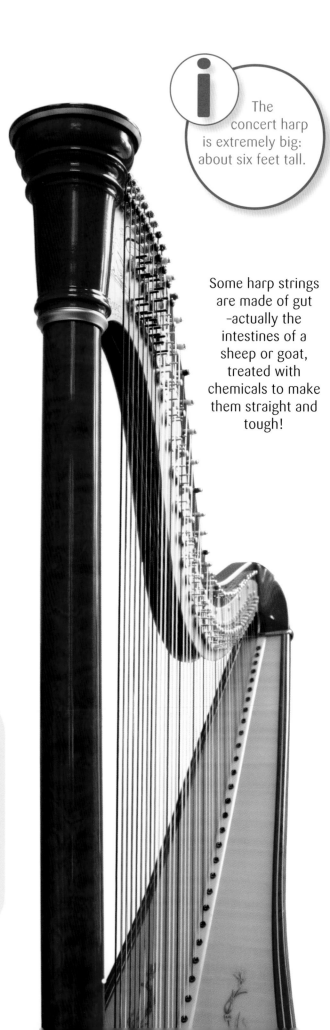

The concert harp is extremely big: about six feet tall.

Some harp strings are made of gut –actually the intestines of a sheep or goat, treated with chemicals to make them straight and tough!

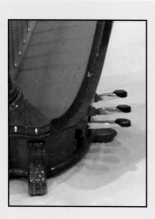

The harp has seven pedals for the feet to press, which can sharpen or flatten the strings by changing their tension. It means a bit of fancy footwork for the harpist, but the result is that the harp can play in any key at all, without needing more strings!

Special Effects

Glissando: This is heard a lot on the harp! The player's hands brush up and down the strings to make a decorative, rippling scale sound.

Harmonics: These are produced by "stopping" the strings with the fingers at certain points. The sound is hollow and less ringing than normal.

Did you know ?

Harp strings can easily snap, sometimes right in the middle of a concert, so players carry extra strings with them.

Highs & Lows
pitch range

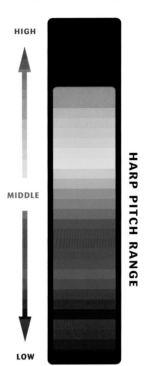

HIGH

MIDDLE

LOW

HARP PITCH RANGE

In the 1940s the harp was so neglected that when the Royal College of Music in London cleared out its instrument collection, 24 harps were chopped up and thrown away! Today they might have been worth $ 1.5 million!

CD-ROM ▶

Hear the instruments! Click Harp Sound under "Strings"

The Marx Brothers were famous showmen of the early 20th century. One of them played the harp very well: he was called 'Harpo' Marx!

The Guitar
Popular Spaniard

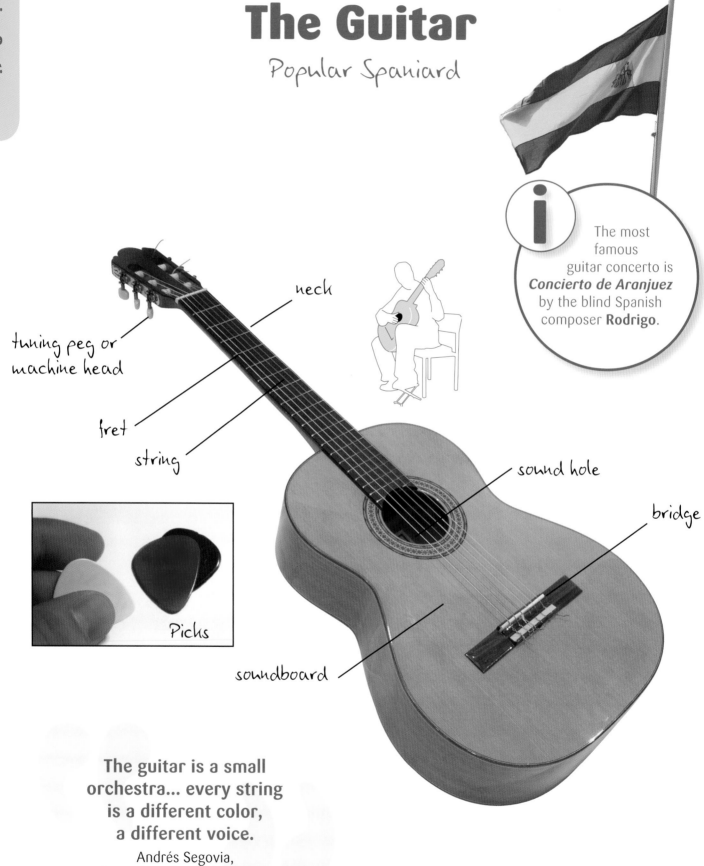

The most famous guitar concerto is *Concierto de Aranjuez* by the blind Spanish composer **Rodrigo**.

neck

tuning peg or machine head

fret

string

sound hole

bridge

Picks

soundboard

The guitar is a small orchestra... every string is a different color, a different voice.

Andrés Segovia,
legendary classical guitarist

Overall

The guitar's main claim to fame is that it gets everywhere! It's in pop, rock, heavy metal, jazz, folk, and more than happy to go solo. There are two main types of guitar.

Acoustic guitars

This group includes the classical guitar (pictured on the opposite page), which has been around for centuries. It's always been a popular instrument in Spain. Many famous guitar makers and players have been Spanish. The famous Italian violin maker Stradivari also made guitars and mandolins.

All acoustic guitars have a hollow, "S"-shaped body of varnished wood in varying shades. There's a big round hole to help the sound (instead of the f-holes on the violin-family instruments).

Electric guitars

These are a modern, 20th-century development. They have a slimmer body and no big round sound hole. When the strings are plucked, they vibrate over tiny coils of wire on magnets. This creates an electrical signal which is passed through an amplifier and comes blasting out of speakers. It's not the kind of guitar Paganini knew about! It's used in rock and pop bands.

How do you play it?

A guitar is always plucked (or sometimes strummed) – there's not a bow in sight. You hold it across your body diagonally, so that your left hand can press the strings on the fingerboard and your right hand can pluck the strings with the fingers or a pick.

The guitar's fingerboard is divided horizontally into sections by thin strips of metal called "frets." This makes it easy to find notes on the strings and therefore to play chords – which guitarists do a lot.

Highs & Lows pitch range

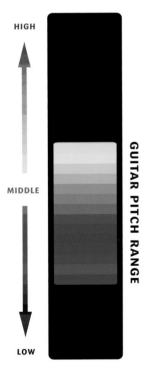

HIGH

MIDDLE

LOW

GUITAR PITCH RANGE

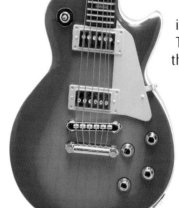

Electric guitar

CD-ROM ▶

Hear the instruments! Click Guitar Sound under "Strings"

The Mandolin
The Lone Tinkler

tuning peg or machine head

string

neck

fret

sound hole

bridge

belly

tailpiece

The word "mandolin" is related to the Italian word for "almond" – "mandorla." The mandolin is shaped like an almond!

This is little-known fact...
but cats like anything in the soprano range. They don't like things that are alto, so you can't play a guitar or a viola to a cat. They just walk out with their tails in the air. But they do like a mandolin.

Louis de Bernières, in his best-selling novel
Captain Corelli's Mandolin

Overall

Dating back 400 years, the mandolin is related to the lute – an early plucked string instrument that used to accompany songs, often sad ones.

In the 20th century, there was a new burst of interest in the mandolin. This was helped by the author Louis de Bernières when he wrote a best-selling novel called *Captain Corelli's Mandolin* – all about an Italian soldier who takes his mandolin everywhere he goes.

The mandolin makes a delicate plinking sound. It used to be plucked with a quill – a feather from an ostrich or a hen. Now it's plucked with a pick.

It has frets, like the guitar, but the strings are in pairs, tuned to the same note. Just as there are electric guitars, there are also electric mandolins.

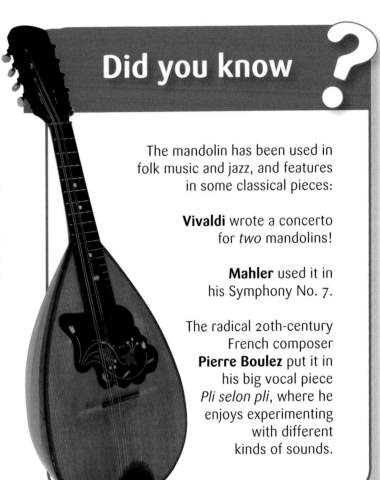

Did you know ?

The mandolin has been used in folk music and jazz, and features in some classical pieces:

Vivaldi wrote a concerto for *two* mandolins!

Mahler used it in his Symphony No. 7.

The radical 20th-century French composer **Pierre Boulez** put it in his big vocal piece *Pli selon pli*, where he enjoys experimenting with different kinds of sounds.

Highs & Lows pitch range

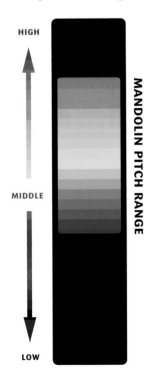

HIGH

MIDDLE

LOW

MANDOLIN PITCH RANGE

How do you play it?

You hold it diagonally across your body, like the guitar.

The idea is to tickle the pick backwards and forwards very fast over each note, to make a tremolo ("trembling") kind of sound.

The fingers of your left hand press the strings in between the frets for different notes.

CD-ROM ▶

Hear the instruments! Click Mandolin Sound under "Strings"

THE WOODWINDS

Each woodwind instrument makes a distinct sound. All are tubes with keys for the fingers and somewhere for the mouth to blow, but they sound completely different!

Long Ago

Woodwind instruments have been around for centuries. Our ancestors may have blown into shells or hollow bits of wood to make sounds, and flutes were certainly present in prehistoric times, made from animal bone.

Oboe   **Flute**   **Clarinet**   **Bassoon**

The Family Members

The **flute**, **oboe**, **clarinet** and **bassoon** are like the primary colors for an artist (the composer) to use. They are the basic sounds available in a symphony orchestra. But adding extra instruments – and therefore extra colors – makes things even more interesting:

In the 17th century, woodwind players could often play more than one instrument. Players were multi-skilled – but the general standard of playing is thought to have been lower than it is today.

Piccolo — a baby flute; sounds higher

English horn — also known as "cor anglais" – an enlarged oboe; sounds lower

Bass clarinet — a big, deep-voiced clarinet, with the bottom bent upwards and the top bent downwards

Contrabassoon — "double bassoon" – nearly twenty feet of tube folded into four parts; sounds lower than a bassoon

Saxophone — the streetwise "Mr Cool" of the woodwind family

Piccolo   **English Horn**   **Bass Clarinet**   **Contrabassoon**   **Saxophone**

In the orchestra...

While string players have safety in numbers - and feel supported during difficult passages - there are fewer woodwind instruments in a typical orchestra. Therefore a woodwind player needs to be calm under pressure to make sure he or she doesn't mess up the solos!

The sound of woodwinds is actually affected by the size and shape of the player's mouth. All players work to adjust the shape to produce the best tone.

Construction of the Instruments

Most woodwinds are, in fact, made of wood, but there are a couple of rebels:

Flutes were made of wood years ago, but now are usually made of metal.

Saxophones are made of brass. But because they have a mouthpiece with a reed, they belong to the woodwind section (and are often played by clarinetists).

How is the sound made?

All woodwind instruments are just tubes with holes! To supply the "wind," the player blows:

Across a hole (flute)
Down a hole (recorder)
On a reed (clarinet, oboe, bassoon)

This makes waves of air vibrate down the tube and come out at the other end as sound. Air comes out through any open key holes too.

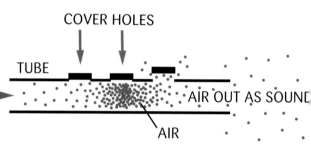

COVER HOLES

TUBE

AIR IN

AIR OUT AS SOUND

AIR

Holes down the length of a tube can be covered and uncovered to make different notes.

The longer the tube, the lower the note.

The shorter the tube, the higher the note.

Clarinet reed

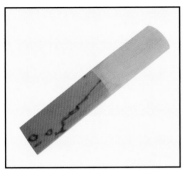

Saxophone reed

Bassoon reed

Oboe reed

Reeds

Clarinets, saxophones, oboes and bassoons use reeds to produce their sound. The clarinet and saxophone have a "single reed"; oboes and bassoons have a "double reed." The type of reed affects the sound, and must suit both the player and the instrument.

Single reed

The simplest sort! One sliver of cane, held onto the instrument's mouthpiece by a metal band. The reed vibrates against the mouthpiece.

Double reed

Two slivers of cane with a base that slots into the instrument. The two slivers vibrate against each other when the player blows on their ends.

Oboes and bassoonists spend a lot of time fiddling with reeds, and if a solo goes wrong it might be the reed's fault! Many don't buy finished reeds: they get the raw cane and have a little tool kit to operate on it and make it just the way they want. During a performance, the reed has to be kept moist.

Did you know?

Reeds don't last forever! After a reed has been used a few times it is likely to split. When that happens, the player will buy or make a new one.

Alike? Not really!

The oboe and clarinet, at first glance, look very similar. But although they're both black tubes covered in silver keys, they're quite different:

Clarinet	Oboe
Single reed	Double reed
Body is cylindrical: the same width all the way down until the bell	Body is more conical – like a cone: gets wider towards the bottom
Smooth, thick sound	Grassy, thin sound
Invented in the 18th century	Its ancestor (shawm) dates back to the 13th century
Used in jazz	Never used in jazz

An older kind of double-tonguing for the flute was known as "tootle-tootle" in English and "didd'l-didd'l" in German.

Special Effects

Double-tonguing: This is a way of playing fast notes, and players often do it by quickly mouthing "T-K-T-K" down the instrument.

Flutter-tonguing: Mainly for the flute, sometimes the clarinet, this is a fluttering kind of sound made by trilling the tongue as you play. The player rolls an "R", with the tongue behind the teeth.

Vibrato: This is where the note is made to wobble just slightly, making the sound a bit richer. You do this either by using your diaphragm (the little muscle at the bottom of your lungs) or moving your bottom lip up and down slightly. How much it's used depends on the instrument, as well as the player's style and the music being played.

Glissando: A swooping effect, up or down.

Woodwinds in the Orchestra

Did you know?

Woodwind players prefer not to be too close to the brass in the orchestra: their ears get blasted and they can't hear what they're doing!

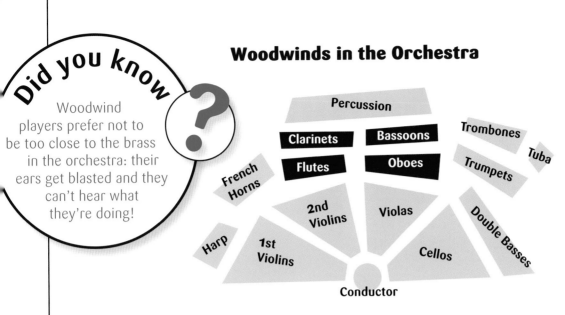

Percussion

Clarinets   Bassoons   Trombones

Flutes   Oboes   Tuba

French Horns   Trumpets

2nd Violins   Violas   Double Basses

Harp   1st Violins   Cellos

Conductor

Like the animals in Noah's Ark, woodwind instruments have often gone two-by-two. Particularly for late-18th-century music, it's normal to find pairs of woodwind instruments in the orchestra (two flutes, two clarinets, two bassoons, two oboes). These days it varies, but a typical line-up is:

2 flutes + 1 piccolo
2 oboes + 1 english horn
2 clarinets + 1 bass clarinet
2 bassoons + 1 contrabassoon

The four main instruments – flute, oboe, clarinet, bassoon – are very different from each other, but all make good solo instruments. Just one can sound clearly right through the orchestra when it is given a melody of its own to play. So orchestral pieces are stacked with great woodwind solos!

As the woodwind players sit behind the strings, they're further away from the conductor and have to watch carefully. But their sound doesn't have any trouble in floating right over the top of the strings and across to the audience.

Playing Together - Chamber Music

Woodwind instruments often play together in groups, especially in wind quintets. These are for flute, oboe, clarinet, bassoon – and French horn. The French horn is officially a brass instrument, but it blends well with the woodwind instruments.

CD-ROM ▶

Hear the instruments! Click Sound under "Woodwind"

The Flute
The Family's Finest Flutterer

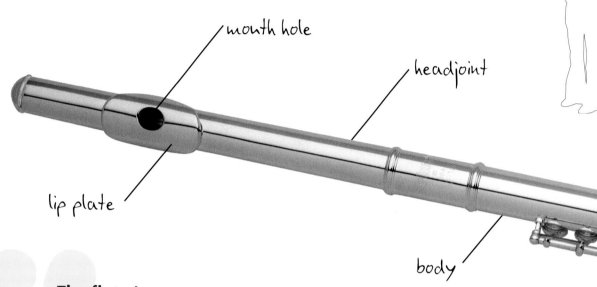

mouth hole

headjoint

lip plate

body

> " **The flute is not an instrument which has a good moral effect. It is too exciting.** "
>
> Aristotle,
> ancient Greek philosopher

Overall

The flute is one of the earliest instruments in the world. It goes right back to the Stone Age, two or three *million* years ago. People discovered that if they made holes in pieces of animal bone, or bark, or shells, they could blow down them and produce notes.

These days, with its shiny metal body and keys, the flute is a long way from a bone with a hole in it. But the idea is the same! Up at the top of the orchestra, with lots of high notes, the flute reigns supreme. It dances so naturally you'd think it could go on for ever. A good flautist can make it sound as if it's the easiest thing in the world. But no instrument is *that* easy – it takes practice, skill and experience.

Flute players are often called **"flautists."**

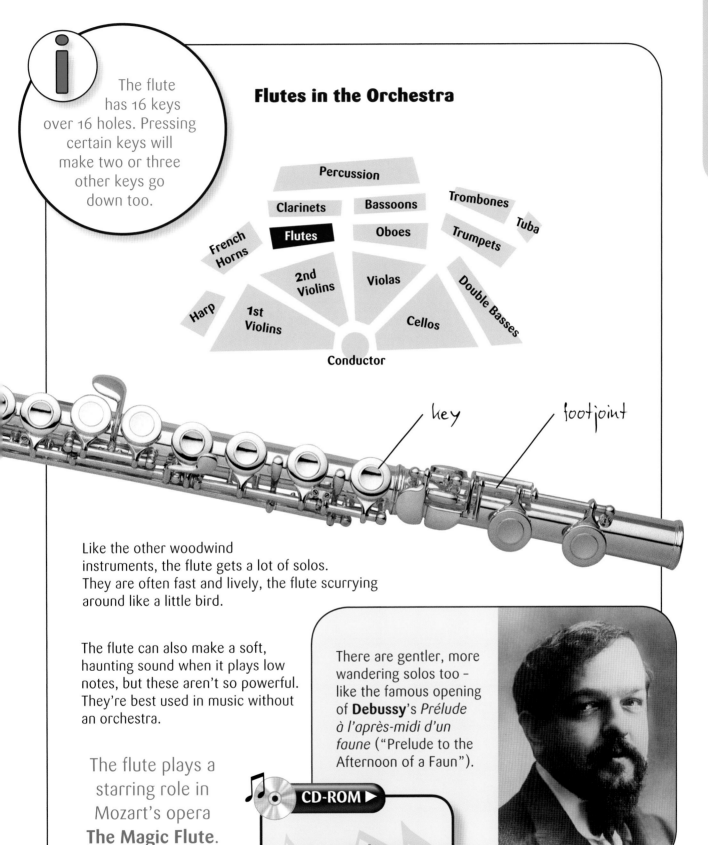

The flute has 16 keys over 16 holes. Pressing certain keys will make two or three other keys go down too.

Flutes in the Orchestra

Percussion

Clarinets   Bassoons   Trombones

French Horns   Flutes   Oboes   Tuba

Trumpets

2nd Violins   Violas   Double Basses

Harp   1st Violins   Cellos

Conductor

key

footjoint

Like the other woodwind instruments, the flute gets a lot of solos. They are often fast and lively, the flute scurrying around like a little bird.

The flute can also make a soft, haunting sound when it plays low notes, but these aren't so powerful. They're best used in music without an orchestra.

The flute plays a starring role in Mozart's opera **The Magic Flute**.

There are gentler, more wandering solos too – like the famous opening of **Debussy**'s *Prélude à l'après-midi d'un faune* ("Prelude to the Afternoon of a Faun").

CD-ROM ▶

Hear Debussy Click Flute Sound under "Woodwind"

It's a fact...

Flutes around the world are blown in different ways. At one time, it was even quite common for the nose to do the blowing instead of the mouth! The instruments were given a fitting name: "nose flutes."

You can find a flute in:

Solo Pieces and Concertos: There are many, especially concertos from the Baroque era (1600–1750). Some solos pair the flute with the piano.

Chamber music: Plenty of chamber music, including wind quintets (flute, oboe, clarinet, bassoon, French horn).

Folk music: Versions of the flute exist around the world, and play all kinds of traditional folk music in other countries and cultures.

Construction of the Flute

- Most flutes are made of silver.
- For players with a lot of money, there are platinum and gold ones.
- **Wooden** ones still exist, too. These are a bit less sparkly in sound, and some players like that.

There are three sections to the flute, which slide together.

1) Headjoint
2) Body
3) Footjoint

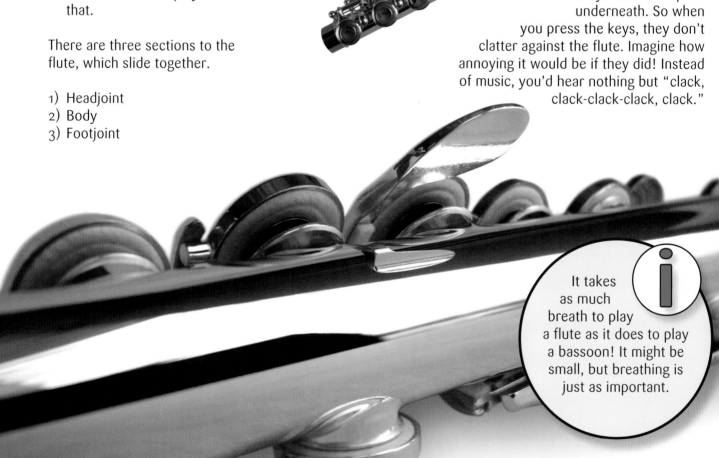

headjoint

footjoint

body

The 16 metal keys have little pads underneath. So when you press the keys, they don't clatter against the flute. Imagine how annoying it would be if they did! Instead of music, you'd hear nothing but "clack, clack-clack-clack, clack."

It takes as much breath to play a flute as it does to play a bassoon! It might be small, but breathing is just as important.

Did you know ?

At London's Great Exhibition in 1851, Theobald Boehm received a gold medal for his redesign of the flute. All the keywork on the modern flute – the way the keys are designed and laid out – is thanks to Mr Boehm.

The tongue is very important for the flute: many notes are begun by pronouncing the letter "T" into the flute a fraction before the breath comes out. This ensures a clean, clear start.

The stream of air that comes out of your mouth splits against the edge of the mouthpiece. This sets vibrations going down the flute... and out comes sound!

The flute and harp are featured in many pieces, like Mozart's fabulous Flute and Harp Concerto. You might not have guessed it, but they actually sound great together.

How do you play it?

Have you ever made a sound by blowing across the top of an empty bottle? Well, that's exactly how you play the flute!

1) You bring the lip plate to your mouth, so that the flute sticks out horizontally to your right.

2) One hand is curled around towards you along one half of the flute; the other hand is curled around away from you along the other half of the flute: in this position, your fingers press keys for different notes.

3) Then you blow across the mouth hole (also called the embouchure hole).

4) Your fingers press keys for different notes.

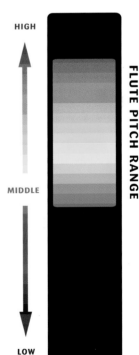

Special Effects

Flutter-tonguing:
The flute's best special effect is "flutter-tonguing." The player rolls an "R", with the tongue behind the teeth, and out comes an exciting, shivery kind of sound.

For more about playing the flute, look at page 54.

CD-ROM ▶

Hear the instruments! Click Flute Sound under "Woodwind"

Highs & Lows pitch range

HIGH

MIDDLE

LOW

FLUTE PITCH RANGE

Other Flutes

Piccolo

The little one! A piccolo is like half a flute: it's half the length and plays an octave higher. Its high, bright little notes can always be heard very clearly above everyone else's: in the orchestra, it's the highest of the high.

Unlike the flute, the piccolo is often made of wood. The wood softens its sharp sound a bit so it doesn't pierce your ears and make you wince.

Composers sometimes mix in the piccolo to alter the sound of another instrument. It's a bit like seasoning your food with salt and pepper. For example, if you put a piccolo [pepper] with a brass instrument [potato], the effect is that the brass instrument [potato] sounds brighter [tastes nicer!].

Highs & Lows pitch range

HIGH

MIDDLE

LOW

PICCOLO PITCH RANGE

i "Piccolo" means "little" in Italian. Piccolo players like to joke that they're the only ones in the orchestra who play an adjective!

Highs & Lows pitch range

HIGH

MIDDLE

LOW

ALTO FLUTE PITCH RANGE

Alto flute

This is a bigger, lower flute. It's not used that much, because it's a bit quiet and gets drowned out by all the others.

It can have a mellow, airy sort of sound - and some composers like to make the most of that.

The flute often stars in folk stories and fairytales. In The Pied Piper of Hamelin, the Pied Piper plays on his pipe, or flute, and the children all follow him.

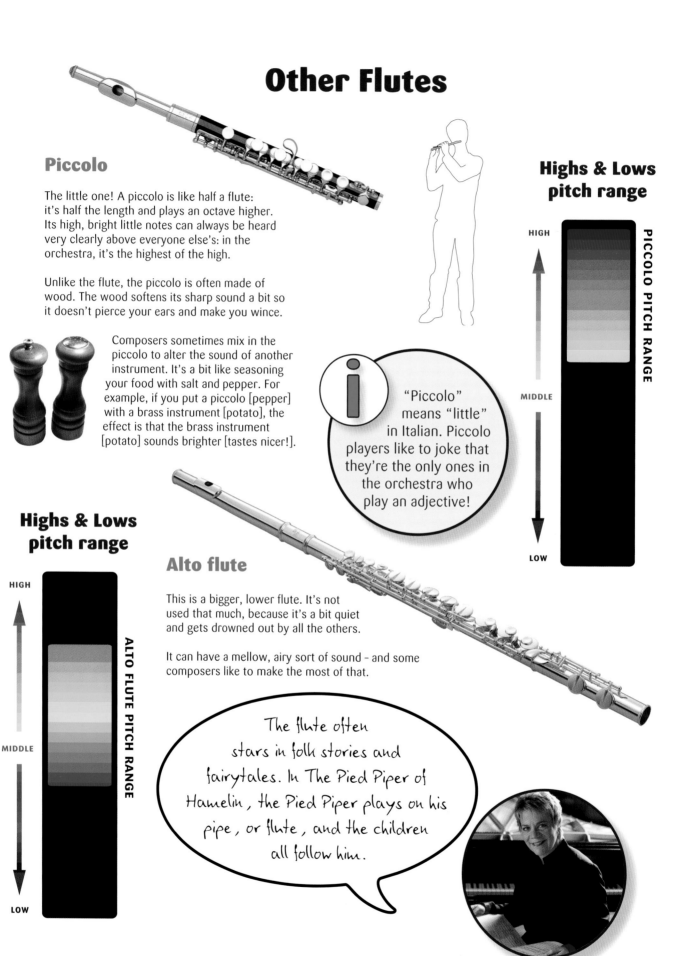

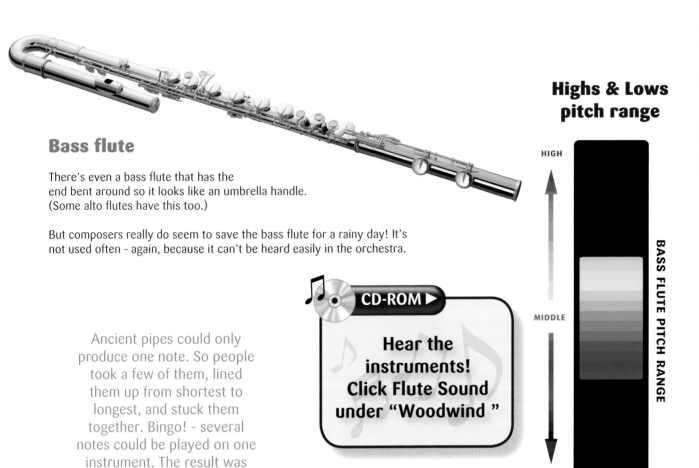

Bass flute

There's even a bass flute that has the
end bent around so it looks like an umbrella handle.
(Some alto flutes have this too.)

But composers really do seem to save the bass flute for a rainy day! It's
not used often - again, because it can't be heard easily in the orchestra.

Ancient pipes could only
produce one note. So people
took a few of them, lined
them up from shortest to
longest, and stuck them
together. Bingo! - several
notes could be played on one
instrument. The result was
called a "**panpipe**."

CD-ROM ▶

**Hear the
instruments!
Click Flute Sound
under "Woodwind "**

Highs & Lows
pitch range

HIGH

MIDDLE

LOW

BASS FLUTE PITCH RANGE

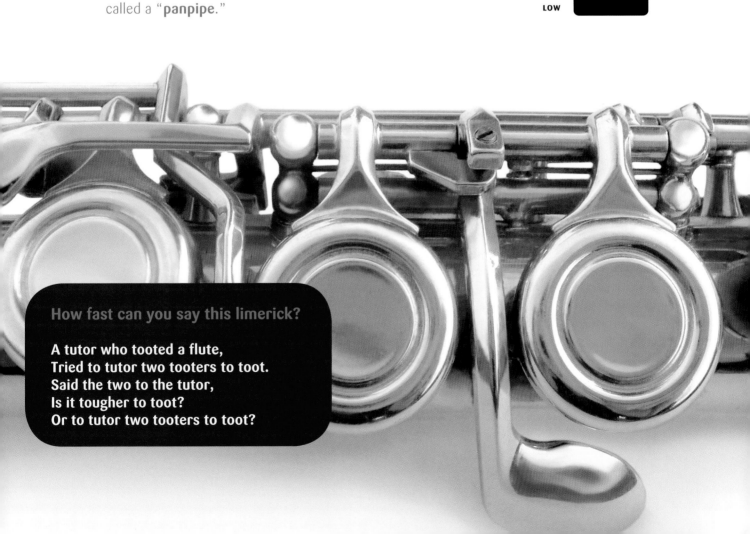

How fast can you say this limerick?

A tutor who tooted a flute,
Tried to tutor two tooters to toot.
Said the two to the tutor,
Is it tougher to toot?
Or to tutor two tooters to toot?

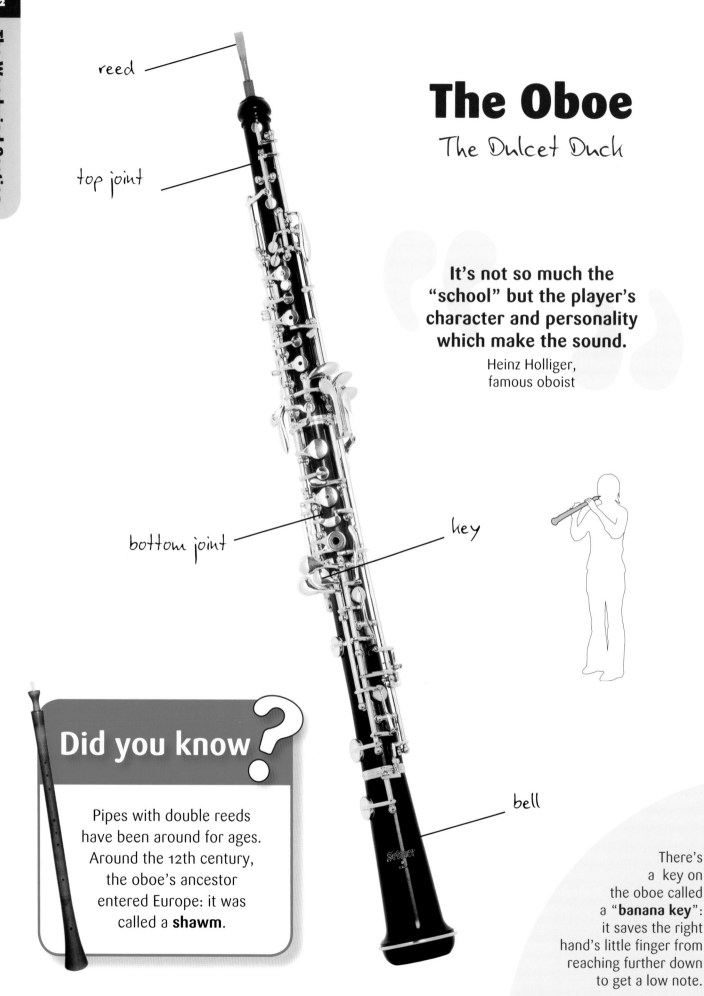

reed

top joint

bottom joint

key

bell

The Oboe
The Dulcet Duck

It's not so much the "school" but the player's character and personality which make the sound.

Heinz Holliger,
famous oboist

Did you know?

Pipes with double reeds have been around for ages. Around the 12th century, the oboe's ancestor entered Europe: it was called a **shawm**.

There's a key on the oboe called a **"banana key"**: it saves the right hand's little finger from reaching further down to get a low note.

Overall

Bright, wistful and crystal clear, the sound of the oboe makes you stop and listen. It's not particularly loud, but its sound seems to cut through the rest of the orchestra and insist on being heard. It's particularly good at playing sad music.

 **CD-ROM ▶**

Hear Prokofiev Click Oboe Sound under "Woodwind"

In his famous piece *Peter and the Wolf*, the composer **Prokofiev** decided that the oboe would be the duck. Ever since, oboists have put up with people saying that their instrument sounds like a duck! It's a slightly nasal and reedy sound, so to make it play the duck was a fun idea. But you have to use your imagination: the oboe is actually much, much more beautiful than a duck's quack, however talented the duck may be.

Oboes in the Orchestra

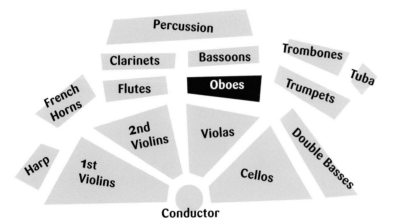

Tuning

Because the oboe can be heard so clearly through the orchestra, it has a starring role right at the start of every concert: it plays a long, loud note by itself. As soon as this note - an "A" - is heard, all the other players have to start concentrating and make sure their instruments are "in tune." This means that *their* "A", on *their* instrument, has to perfectly match the oboe's "A". It mustn't be a fraction sharper (higher) or flatter (lower).

The sound of the orchestra "tuning up" is very easy to recognize: all instruments playing mostly one note, perhaps a few others, and no rules for when to start and stop. It's like birds in a cage!

What if the oboist's "A" is wrong? It never is: the oboist uses a "tuning fork" first, to make sure the "A" is right.

A **tuning fork** is like an over-sized dinner fork with only two, blunt prongs. You tap it against something hard (even your head or knee, if you're feeling tough!) to make it vibrate. Then you put it to your ear and listen: it produces a perfect "A". A tuning fork never goes out of tune, so the oboist can always rely on it. Once the oboe matches the fork, the orchestra can match the oboe – and the music can begin...

Tuning fork

The word "**oboe**" comes from the French word "**hautbois**," meaning "**high wood**": the oboe is a high-pitched instrument made out of wood.

The Music

In orchestral pieces, the oboe is at its best when it has solos to play. Mainly, it sounds:

1) Sad
2) Energetic

When it has long lines of melody, it can sound very expressive. It almost seems to cast a spell on the listener: when it sounds sad, *you* feel sad too. This happens with other instruments, but especially with the oboe.

When it's full of energy, it's like a little pixie, dashing around, light-footed and playful.

You can find oboes in:

Concertos: Quite a lot, mainly from either the Baroque era (1600–1750) or the 20th century.

Chamber music: Mostly wind quintets (flute, oboe, clarinet, bassoon, French horn) but other combinations as well.

Solo pieces: Many from the Baroque era and 20th century.

Construction of the Oboe

The oboe's **body** is made of hard, black wood – African blackwood, rosewood or ebonite. Some modern ones are made from plastic: not lunchbox kind of plastic, but hard and black so it looks like wood.

The oboe has often been used to suggest **outdoor scenes.** Beethoven used it that way in his "Pastoral" Symphony, and Grieg in his *Peer Gynt*. Funny, since it was specifically designed as an indoor instrument when its predecessor, the shawm, sounded too harsh!

Oboists can often be seen sucking their reed as if it were a lollipop. It's because it has to remain moist to stay flexible.

The **keys** are metal. The **reed** is a "double-reed": two very thin slices of cane that vibrate against each other when the oboe is played.

Players make their own reeds. They carry a miniature tool kit wherever they go, ready to sit for hours and scrape slivers of cane. Oboists might seem fussy, but they have good reason: their reed can help them sound brilliant... or terrible.

The oboe splits into three parts: the top joint, the bottom joint and the bell.

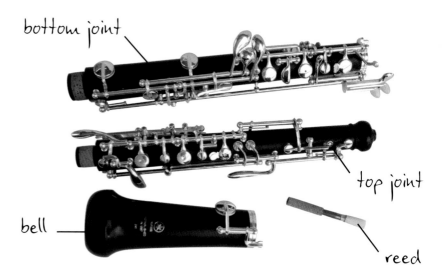

bottom joint

top joint

bell

reed

The main makers are French and German. Both have made oboes over the years which are slightly different but equally good.

How do you play it?

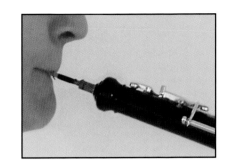

Basically, you:

1) Pick it up.
2) Put your lips around the reed.
3) Take a deep breath.
4) Blow... but not too hard.

Although you need a lot of air inside you to play the oboe, the amount that comes out when you play is very small. So oboists don't just breathe *in* every so often, they breathe *out* too, to get rid of the breath they haven't used.

They also do "circular breathing," which is what glassblowers do: you blow out through your mouth while breathing in through your nose. Try it! It's not easy... you have to learn how to do it.

Like other wind instruments, a column of air vibrates through the oboe and comes out as sound. You press keys for different notes. But it isn't an easy instrument to control! The beautiful, clear sound that it can make takes a long time to master.

For more about playing the oboe, look at page 54.

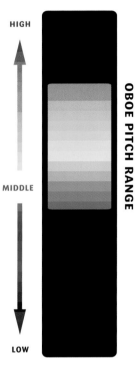

Highs & Lows pitch range

HIGH

MIDDLE

LOW

OBOE PITCH RANGE

Oboe keys might *look* complicated, but they're not really. A lot of the metal is just for extensions, so that the bottom keys can be activated without players straining their fingers. They simply press keys further up, and these make the bottom keys work.

Other Oboes

English Horn
or "cor anglais"

This is a deep-voiced oboe. It's often used in the orchestra to play sorrowful, lonely melodies.

Because it's bigger than an oboe, it isn't lifted as high when it's played: the reed is angled out towards the player instead of just poking out at the top. The bell at the bottom is shaped like a pear.

Its sound is even harder to control than the oboe's, so players need strong nerves to play the solos. Sometimes, there you are, in the middle of a gorgeous, tear-jerking melody, and... "crack"... a note "breaks" and ruins the mood.

> i "Cor anglais" is French and means "**English horn**" – but the instrument is neither English nor a horn. How confusing! The name is thought to have come from "cor anglé" – meaning "angled horn" – which sounds the same but makes more sense.

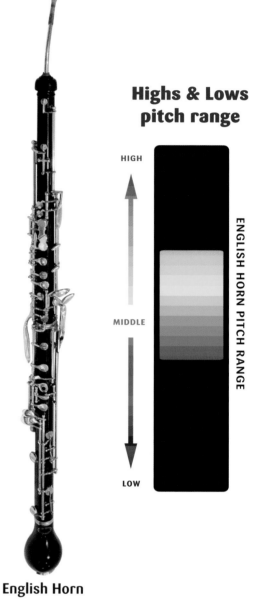

Highs & Lows pitch range

HIGH

MIDDLE

LOW

ENGLISH HORN PITCH RANGE

English Horn

Bass oboe

Even lower than the English horn, and not used much.

Heckelphone

A badly designed bass oboe! Strauss sometimes used it in his operas, but most other composers wisely left it alone.

Oboe d'amore

This is in between the oboe and the English horn in pitch. It looks like a English horn, with its angled mouthpiece and pear-shaped bell.

Its name means "oboe of love" – and Bach loved it! He wrote some beautiful melodies for it in the Baroque era. Since then it's been used much less, though it does appear in **Ravel's** famous *Boléro*.

Oboe d'amore

CD-ROM ▶

Hear the instruments! Click Oboe Sound under "Woodwind"

mouthpiece

barrel

top joint

key

bottom joint

The Clarinet
Cool Cat

In Prokofiev's *Peter and the Wolf*, the clarinet is a cat – and the comparison is perfect! It's a sleek and agile instrument that can slide carefully through its slow bits and pounce on its fast ones.

It may have been called a "**clarinet**" because its top notes sounded a bit like a **trumpet**. A "**clarion**" was an early trumpet – and "**clarionet**" means "little trumpet."

The American film director **Woody Allen** is a good jazz clarinettist. He has his own New Orleans Jazz Band.

bell

Overall

The clarinet is quite a young instrument. It was invented in about 1700.
That might *seem* like a long time ago – it *is* a long time ago – but flutes,
oboes and bassoons had been tootling away for years by that time.

Clarinets can express themselves very well: their low notes (very low!) are dark and moody; their high notes (very high!) are bright and shrill. They can be hushed and mellow, or loud and penetrating. Overall, the sound is smooth and velvety.

Like the violin in the string family, the clarinet is the most versatile member of the woodwind family. This means that it can make lots of different sounds and whizz around all over the place – from top to bottom, bottom to top – perhaps with a few twiddles along the way.

> The sound produced on the clarinet is actually affected by the shape and size of the player's mouth.

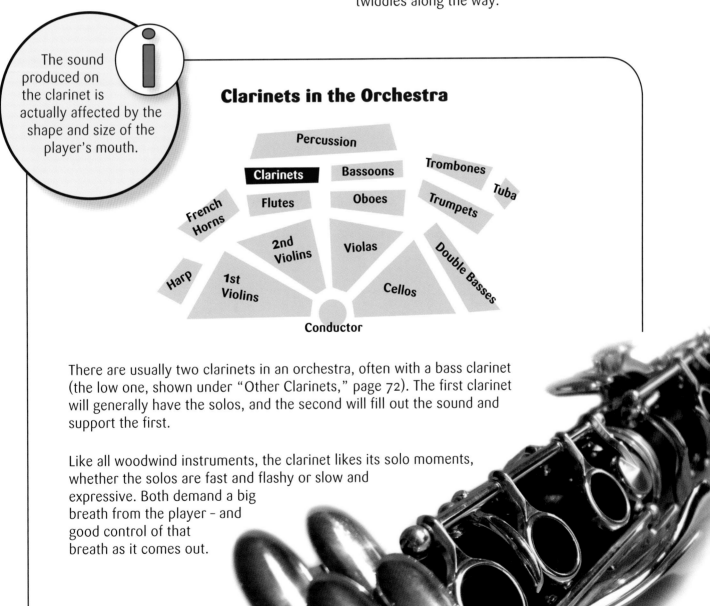

Clarinets in the Orchestra

Percussion

Clarinets   Bassoons

French Horns   Flutes   Oboes   Trombones   Tuba   Trumpets

Harp   1st Violins   2nd Violins   Violas   Cellos   Double Basses

Conductor

There are usually two clarinets in an orchestra, often with a bass clarinet (the low one, shown under "Other Clarinets," page 72). The first clarinet will generally have the solos, and the second will fill out the sound and support the first.

Like all woodwind instruments, the clarinet likes its solo moments, whether the solos are fast and flashy or slow and expressive. Both demand a big breath from the player – and good control of that breath as it comes out.

The clarinet fits into a variety of situations:

CD-ROM ▶

Concertos: Mozart wrote the most famous one, but there are many others for the clarinet. Click Clarinet Sound under "Woodwind" to listen.

Chamber music: Clarinets sound wonderful in chamber music, and work well with many other instruments.

Solo pieces: Many, for clarinet alone or clarinet with piano.

Jazz: The clarinet is perfect for producing the typically rhythmic, swooping, rippling sounds of traditional jazz and swing music, which grew up in the mid-20th century.

World music: The clarinet is used in klezmer music (a type of traditional Jewish music) as well as in the folk music of Greece and Turkey, among other countries.

How do you play it?

Acker Bilk, a leading jazz clarinetist, lost two front teeth in a fight at school, then lost half a finger in a sledging accident. But he was still a great player! He made his name with a little piece called *Stranger on the Shore.*

1) You put your mouth around the mouthpiece so that your bottom lip is touching the reed, take a deep breath... and blow!
2) You control how fast the breath comes out of your mouth by using your diaphragm – a large, dome-shaped muscle underneath your lungs.
3) The reed vibrates on the mouthpiece which sends waves of vibrating air down the body of the clarinet.
4) This air then comes out of the bell at the end as a sound. Sound comes out of the body of the clarinet, too – through the holes.
5) Your fingers press different keys to play different notes.

COVER HOLES

AIR

AIR IN →

AIR OUT AS SOUND

Special Effects

Glissando
The clarinet's best effect is a sliding sound called glissando. There's a fantastic, famous one right at the beginning of Gershwin's *Rhapsody in Blue* where the clarinet swoops up from low to high in a thrilling, unbroken line. It's like a curve in sound! You don't know where it's going to stop, but suddenly it lands perfectly on the note it was aiming for, and everything makes sense.

Flutter-tonguing
Clarinetists can "flutter-tongue" too, and very occasionally they'll use "double-tonguing" for a fast passage (see page 54).

CD-ROM ▶

Hear *Rhapsody in Blue* Click Clarinet Sound under "Woodwind"

Construction of the Clarinet

The **body** of a clarinet is now made out of African blackwood – very hard, very dark wood. It has what is called a "cylindrical bore." This means that it's the same width all the way down, like a pipe, until the open bell at the end.

The **keys** are metal.

On the mouthpiece is a little cane **reed**.

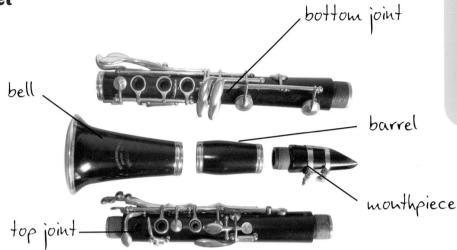

The clarinet is a "single-reed" instrument. The reed is just one thin sliver, held on the mouthpiece by a metal band called a "ligature." Unlike oboists and bassoonists, clarinetists don't need to make their own reeds.

There are five pieces of a clarinet which all fit together to make one long tube.

This means the clarinet can be packed away neatly in a small case when it's not being played.

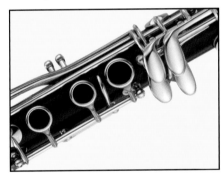

Body made from African blackwood

The bell is made from a block of wood

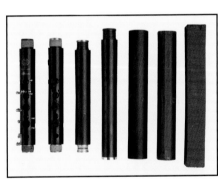

Metal keys

Mouthpiece with reed

Other Clarinets

There are lots of them! The choice of sizes, particularly between A and B flat, makes it easier to play music in different keys.

Clarinet in E flat
(sounds quite high)

Clarinet in B flat
(the usual one)

Clarinet in A

Basset horn

Bass clarinet
(the low one)

Did you know ?

There used to be a wooden instrument called the **chalumeau** - like a recorder but with a single reed on the mouthpiece. In about 1700, a man from Nuremberg called Johann Denner added an important metal key to the chalumeau. This was the birth of the clarinet! The key was called a "speaker key" and meant you could play much higher than before.

Highs & Lows pitch range

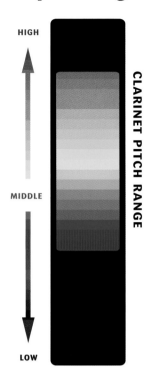

HIGH

MIDDLE

LOW

CLARINET PITCH RANGE

Highs & Lows pitch range

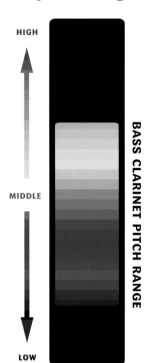

HIGH

MIDDLE

LOW

BASS CLARINET PITCH RANGE

CD-ROM ▶

Hear the instruments! Click Clarinet Sound under "Woodwind"

Mozart loved the slightly deeper sound of the basset horn. He actually wrote his Clarinet Concerto for it, though the piece is usually played today on a regular clarinet.

Basset horn

The basset horn is "in F." This means that it's bigger and sounds lower than the B flat clarinet but is smaller and sounds higher than the bass clarinet.

It has an upturned bell and its mouthpiece comes out just a little way towards the player.

Bass clarinet

This is the big daddy of the clarinet family. The bass clarinet is twice as long as the B flat clarinet. It has a stand to support it on the ground, then an upturned metal bell at the bottom. Its mouthpiece is curved towards the player like a duck's head.

It really can go low: some of its notes are extraordinary and spine-tingling. But it doesn't just grumble underneath the rest of the orchestra: it gets its own solo moments too.

There's even a contrabass clarinet, which goes lower still! But it appears more in wind bands than in orchestras.

The Bassoon

"I'm not a clown!"

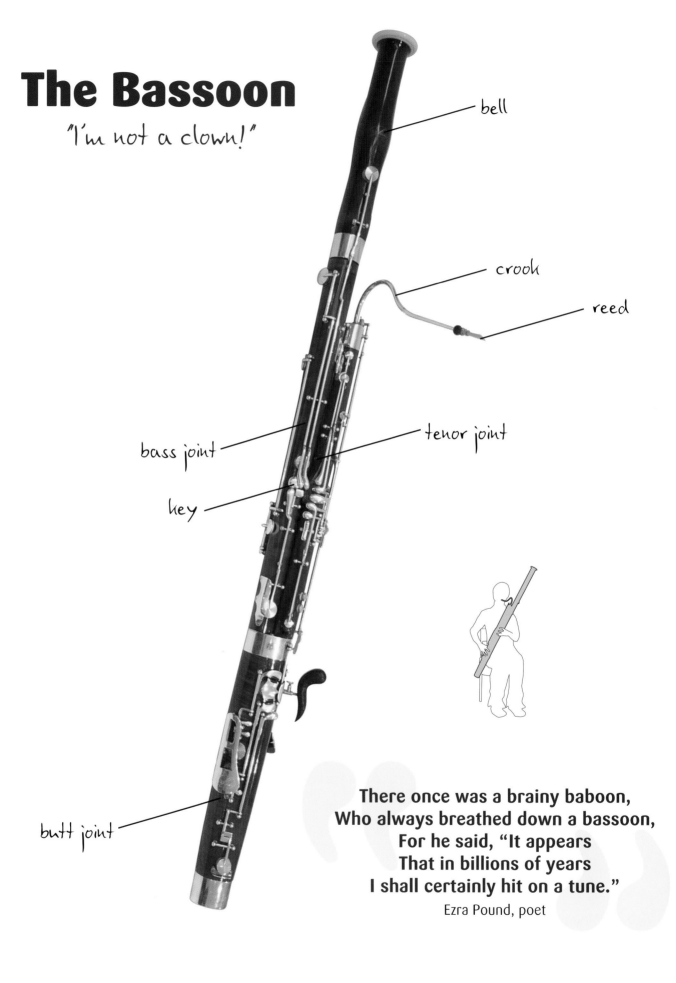

bell

crook

reed

bass joint

tenor joint

hey

butt joint

There once was a brainy baboon,
Who always breathed down a bassoon,
For he said, "It appears
That in billions of years
I shall certainly hit on a tune."

Ezra Pound, poet

Overall

It might be a bass instrument, but the bassoon does more than bumble along a bass line. It gives the underneath of pieces a special character. When it's combined with cellos, for example, its low, dry sound makes the bottom line strong and full of character.

Some people have said the bassoon sounds like an oboe with a cold, but that's a bit mean! In its middle register (when it's playing a bit higher up), it has a lovely, singing sound – like the human tenor voice. Thanks to that, it gets some satisfying solos to play. It's not a show-off, but it's quietly confident about what it can do.

When it goes even higher, it can sound as if it's crying. It can go surprisingly high for such a big instrument. Stravinsky gives its top notes a real workout at the beginning of his *Rite of Spring*.

CD-ROM ▶

**Hear
The Rite of Spring
Click Bassoon
Sound under
"Woodwind"**

Bassoons in the Orchestra

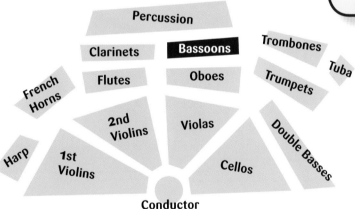

There are normally a couple of bassoons in the orchestra, and they have two main roles:

1) **"Doubling" bass lines:** The cellos might have a line of music in the bass which the bassoons will play as well, making it sound stronger.

2) **Solos:** When it's not playing very low down, the bassoon makes a smooth and gentle solo instrument.

There's also a contrabassoon, which you can meet under "Other Bassoons." This is *really* low. It's like the roots of a tree, supporting everyone else.

Did you know ?

The bassoon got a name for itself as a bit of a clown. It can sound quite funny when it plays bouncy bottom notes – they sound something like "bob-bob-bob." It even plays a grumbling grandfather in Prokofiev's *Peter and the Wolf*. So it has to work hard to make people believe that it isn't *just* a bumbling buffoon!

You can also find bassoons in:

Chamber music: Most often found in wind quintets (flute, oboe, clarinet, bassoon, French horn).

Concertos: Vivaldi wrote 39 bassoon concertos. Only one by Mozart exists, but it's one of the best.

CD-ROM ▶

Listen to Mozart's Bassoon Concerto Click Bassoon Sound under "Woodwind"

Construction of the Bassoon

Bassoons are typically made of maple wood. Four sections are bound together with metal rings: tenor joint (sometimes called "wing" joint), butt joint (double joint), bass joint (long joint), and bell.

bell

tenor joint

bass joint

butt joint

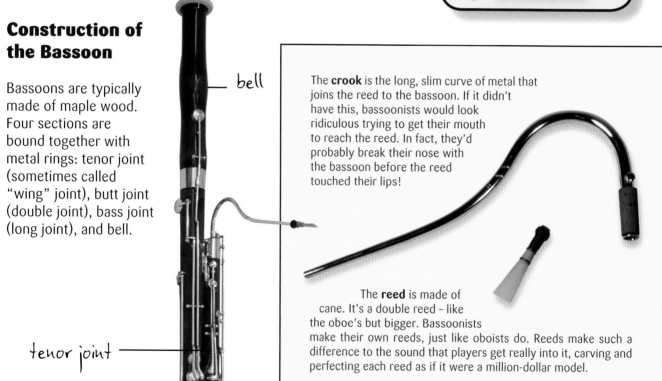

The **crook** is the long, slim curve of metal that joins the reed to the bassoon. If it didn't have this, bassoonists would look ridiculous trying to get their mouth to reach the reed. In fact, they'd probably break their nose with the bassoon before the reed touched their lips!

The **reed** is made of cane. It's a double reed – like the oboe's but bigger. Bassoonists make their own reeds, just like oboists do. Reeds make such a difference to the sound that players get really into it, carving and perfecting each reed as if it were a million-dollar model.

> Some people crave baseball – I find this unfathomable but I can easily understand why a person could get excited about playing a bassoon.

Frank Zappa, American composer, rock musician and guitarist

How do you play it?

With difficulty! The bassoon's design is actually quite silly. It has many things about it which make it tricky to control and play well.

You play it in a very similar way to an oboe, except that you hold it diagonally across yourself. Players have a sling to support it, as it's quite heavy.

Once you blow on the reed, the vibrating air passes through the crook, travels quickly through the joints (tenor → butt → bass), and pops out through the bell at the top. The bell faces the ceiling. Air also comes out through open key holes.

For more about playing the bassoon, look at page 54.

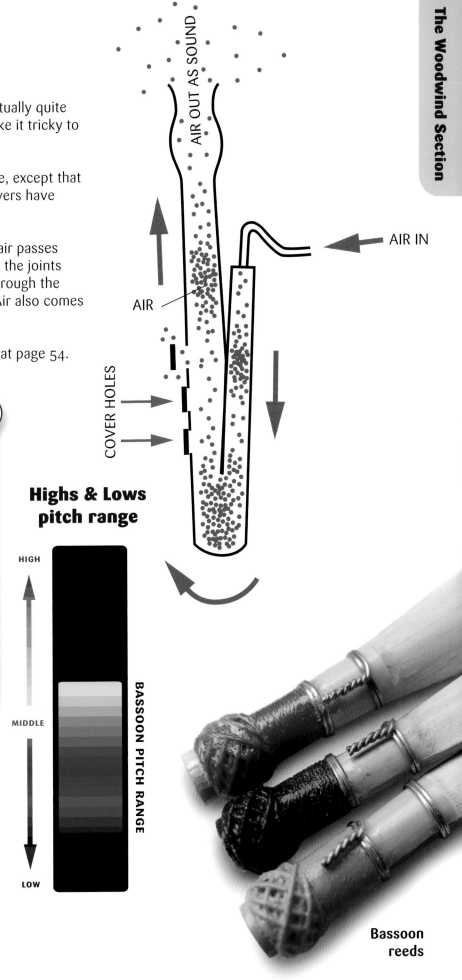

AIR OUT AS SOUND

AIR IN

AIR

COVER HOLES

Did you know?

French and German makers developed the bassoon differently as they did with oboes. Even today, the two types sound quite distinct. German bassoons are seen more often than French ones.

Every single bassoon is a bit different. If something goes wrong with a bassoon, a player can't simply pick up another one and expect to sound the same.

Highs & Lows pitch range

HIGH

MIDDLE

LOW

BASSOON PITCH RANGE

Bassoon reeds

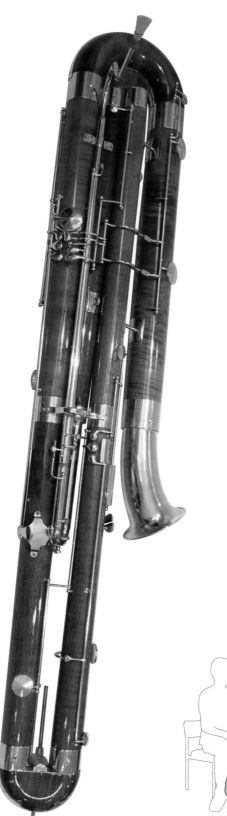

Contrabassoon

Other Bassoons

Contrabassoon
or "double bassoon"

This is an enormous bassoon with fat tubes folded into four parts. It sounds very deep and plays very low down in the orchestra.

Unlike the bassoon, the bell of the contrabassoon faces the floor. And there's a spike on the bottom of the instrument to prop it up on the ground, as it's too heavy to hold in the air.

Tenoroon
or "mini bassoon"

This is like a "baby" bassoon, smaller than a standard bassoon. Because of their size, tenoroons are frequently played by children, but don't often appear in orchestral pieces.

Did you know?

If you stretched out a contrabassoon, it would be over 19 feet long!

Family Highs & Lows - Pitch Ranges Together

Below, you can see how the orchestral woodwind family fits together, from top to bottom.

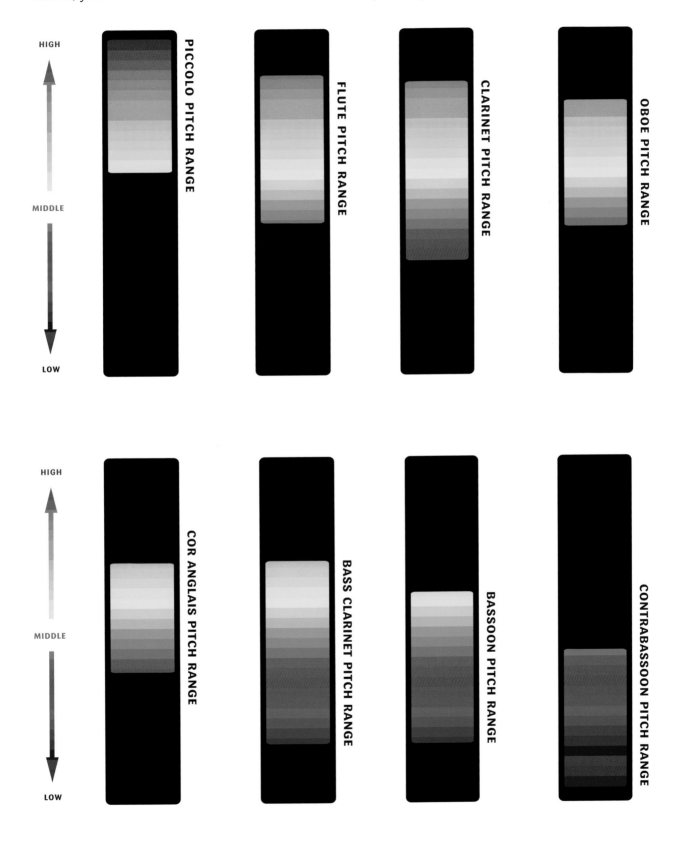

HIGH

MIDDLE

LOW

PICCOLO PITCH RANGE

FLUTE PITCH RANGE

CLARINET PITCH RANGE

OBOE PITCH RANGE

HIGH

MIDDLE

LOW

COR ANGLAIS PITCH RANGE

BASS CLARINET PITCH RANGE

BASSOON PITCH RANGE

CONTRABASSOON PITCH RANGE

mouthpiece

crook

body

key

The Saxophone
Relaxed Rebel

**Don't play the saxophone.
Let it play you.**
Charlie Parker,
jazz saxophonist

bell

i A saxophone
once owned by the
famous jazz saxophonist
Charlie Parker was sold for
$144,500 at Christie's in South
Kensington, London, in 1994.

Overall

"**Saxophone**" is often shortened to
"**sax**." Saxophones are made of brass.
So why aren't they classified as brass
instruments? Two reasons: 1) A sax has
a mouthpiece like the clarinet's, with a
cane reed. 2) It sounds like a woodwind
instrument, not a brass one.

Saxophones in the Orchestra

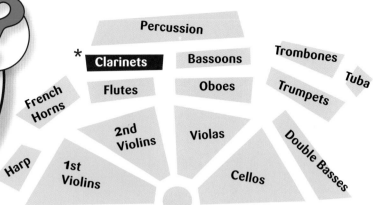

Percussion

* **Clarinets**   Bassoons   Trombones   Tuba

French Horns   Flutes   Oboes   Trumpets

Harp   1st Violins   2nd Violins   Violas   Double Basses   Cellos

Conductor

The saxophone isn't a regular member of the orchestra. Only a few pieces include it. When it's in the orchestra, it adds an unusual, soft-edged sound to the mixture.

When it's in the orchestra, the saxophone adds an unusual, soft-edged sound to the mixture.

*The saxophone sits with the clarinets.

The sax is common in pop music and jazz.

It adores the freedom and the spotlight, and can also play slow, oozing melodies.

It can do all kinds of clever runs up and down. People "improvise" on it. This means they play as the mood takes them: no music, no memory, no plan – just pick it up and go.

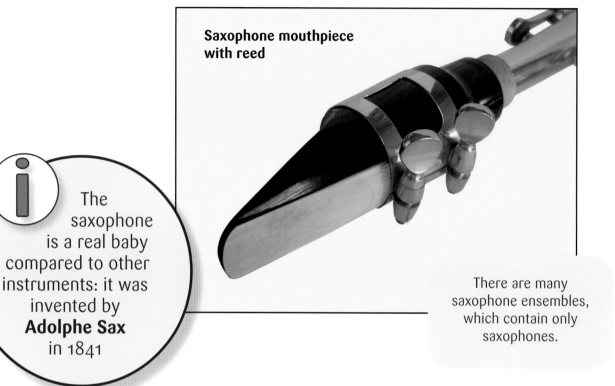

Saxophone mouthpiece
with reed

The
saxophone
is a real baby
compared to other
instruments: it was
invented by
Adolphe Sax
in 1841

There are many
saxophone ensembles,
which contain only
saxophones.

How do you play it?

Just like the clarinet – but it's a bit easier!

It couldn't replace the clarinet, because
the sound is very different. But many
clarinetists also play the saxophone.

Special Effects

The saxophone is great at fooling
around and making funny noises. It
can do glissando, like the clarinet, and
flutter-tonguing, like the flute. It can
even growl, bend, wobble and laugh!

Highs & Lows
pitch range

There are several saxophones!
Here are the ranges of three
familiar ones.

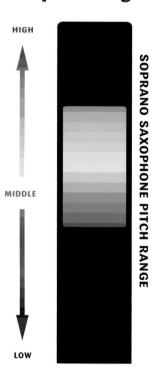

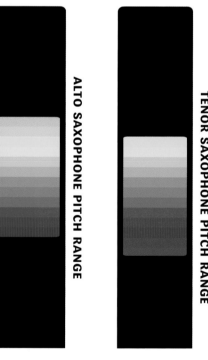

HIGH

MIDDLE

LOW

SOPRANO SAXOPHONE PITCH RANGE

ALTO SAXOPHONE PITCH RANGE

TENOR SAXOPHONE PITCH RANGE

Other Saxophones

Saxophones need a lot of room when the whole family gets together because there are many of them. Once upon a time, there were actually 14 different sizes! Now, things are a bit more sensible and it's come down to eight. In size order:

CD-ROM ▶

Hear the instruments! Click Saxophone Sound under "Woodwind"

Sopranino
Soprano
Alto
Tenor in C ("C-melody" sax)
Tenor in B flat
Baritone
Bass
Contrabass

Former President Bill Clinton plays the saxophone.

Sopranino **Soprano** **Alto** **Tenor** **Baritone** **Bass**

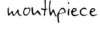

mouthpiece

finger hole

The Recorder
Tootler from Times Past

The recorder is very old. It was certainly played in the 1300s, and in the 1600s it was all over the place. But the flute became a bigger and better rival and overtook the recorder in the mid-1700s.

So the recorder doesn't feature in modern orchestras. But it's still played. It has two main roles:

1) The soprano recorder is often a child's first instrument because it's quite simple to learn. Perhaps you know how to play it?

2) When people want to play music written a long time ago, they like to make it sound as it would have done at the time. So if you want to play a piece written in 1696 for the recorder, you need a recorder to play it! If you play it on a flute, it won't sound "authentic."

The recorder isn't very loud. It simply couldn't compete with the big, powerful instruments that were made in the 18th century.

But when recorders play together, they make a cheerful, bright, clear sound. Many people still play in recorder groups, and many others listen to them. These groups are called "**consorts**."

i

The recorder is a distant relation of the flute. In some countries it's called a "block flute" because it has a block of wood at the mouthpiece end.

Bass   Tenor   Alto   Soprano   Sopranino

Great bass

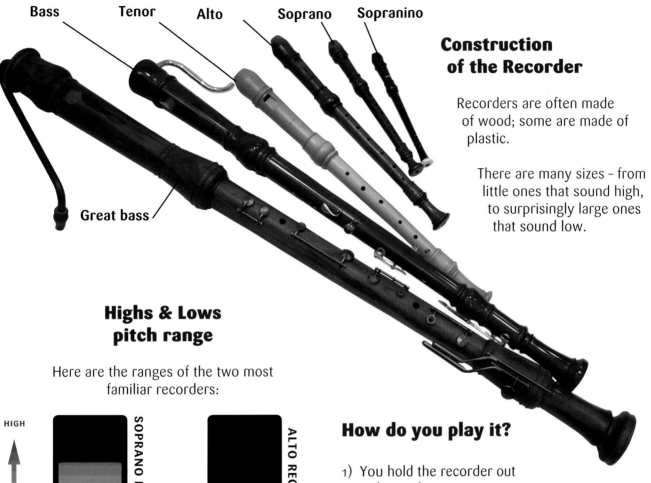

Construction of the Recorder

Recorders are often made of wood; some are made of plastic.

There are many sizes – from little ones that sound high, to surprisingly large ones that sound low.

Highs & Lows pitch range

Here are the ranges of the two most familiar recorders:

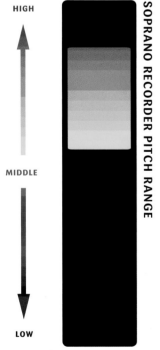

HIGH

MIDDLE

LOW

SOPRANO RECORDER PITCH RANGE

ALTO RECORDER PITCH RANGE

Soprano recorder
The little one that a lot of children play at school.

Alto recorder
The most popular member of the family.

How do you play it?

1) You hold the recorder out in front of you.
2) You blow into the mouthpiece.
3) Your fingers cover different holes for different notes.

According to the American Recorder Society, **March** is "**Play-the-Recorder**" month.

CD-ROM ▶

Hear the instruments! Click Recorder Sound under "Woodwind"

THE BRASS

Brass instruments are powerful and grand, as well as bright and shiny.

Long Ago

Ancestors of the brass family first appeared thousands of years earlier: man chopped the ends off animal horns and blew down them.

In Roman times, they were used as **signaling instruments**. Signals were often used for military events and were sounded on long, simple brass tubes without keys or valves.

The family became known as the "brass" family because the instruments began to be made of metal - usually brass.

Trumpet

Trombone

All brass instruments are **folded** or **coiled** around. This is because they'd be too long to handle if they were stretched out straight. Air doesn't mind going around corners if they're smooth, so the bends and twists don't affect the sound.

French Horn

Tuba

It's a fact...

When you blow down a brass instrument, you put your lips against the mouthpiece. You don't put them around it as you do on woodwind instruments.

Construction of the Instruments

Today, all brass instruments:

...are **wind** instruments.
...are made from **metal**.
...have a **cup-** or **funnel-shaped mouthpiece**.

Sometimes, the brass is silver-plated. If not, it's coated in a special varnish called lacquer which protects the metal and keeps it gleaming.

Some really fancy trumpets are *gold*-plated, and the famous trumpeter Wynton Marsalis has diamonds in his trumpet!

How is the sound made?

- When the player blows into the mouthpiece, the lips vibrate - like blowing a raspberry except with the tongue behind the front teeth.
- This creates waves of vibrating air.
- The vibrating air waves travel through the instrument and come out of the bell at the end as sound.

Mutes

Mutes are put into the bell of brass instruments to soften and change the sound. They're usually made of metal or wood, and shaped like some sort of distorted pear.

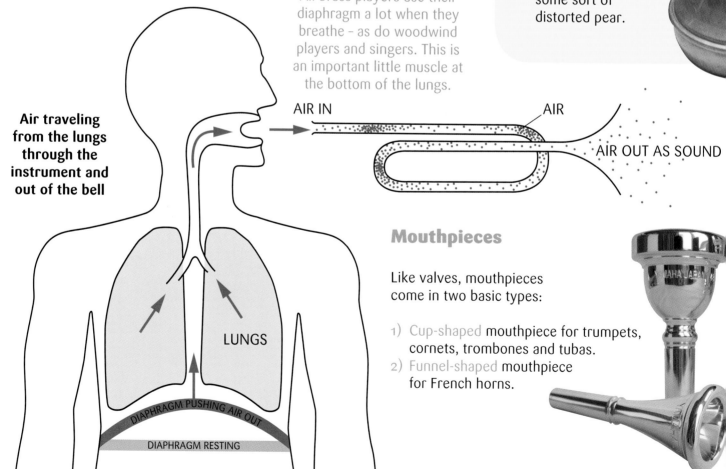

All brass players use their diaphragm a lot when they breathe - as do woodwind players and singers. This is an important little muscle at the bottom of the lungs.

AIR IN   AIR

AIR OUT AS SOUND

Air traveling from the lungs through the instrument and out of the bell

LUNGS

DIAPHRAGM PUSHING AIR OUT

DIAPHRAGM RESTING

Mouthpieces

Like valves, mouthpieces come in two basic types:

1) Cup-shaped mouthpiece for trumpets, cornets, trombones and tubas.
2) Funnel-shaped mouthpiece for French horns.

Pitch

The pitch – how high or low the notes are – depends on:

1) How fast the lips vibrate.
2) The length of the tube.

The trombone has a **slide** – a U-shaped tube – which can move up and down. It alters the total length of the instrument so different pitches can sound.

For brass instruments, like woodwind, pitch depends on the length of the tube. This is why valves and slides were invented – they could change the length of the tube so that different pitches (notes) could be played.

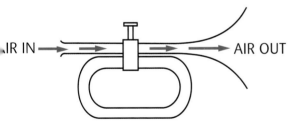

Trombone slide

A French horn has the simplest mute: the player's hand! You couldn't really stick your hand into any of the others because they're so long that the bell is too far away to reach while playing. The horn is curled around neatly, so this isn't a problem.

Horns, trumpets and tubas have **valves** – like the trombone's slide, valves alter the length of the main brass tube so that more notes are possible.

The two types of valves are quite similar:
1) Piston valves are usually for trumpets, cornets and tubas.
2) Rotary valves are for French horns (and some tubas as well).

Piston valves

Rotary valves

AIR IN → → → AIR OUT

PRESS DOWN
↓
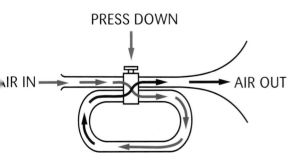
AIR IN → → AIR OUT

Air being diverted by valve

Waves of vibrating air are sent down the instrument when the player blows into the mouthpiece. But the air is diverted by the **valves** – like a train at a railroad switch track. The path of the air changes, and it's sent into separate loops before it's expelled through the bell. This changes the pitch of the note.

In the 17th and 18th centuries, before valves, some brass instruments were given "**crooks.**" These were extra bits of tubing to be added on and taken away so that more notes could be played. But it was a clumsy system.

Special Effects

There are many special ways to play brass instruments. These are the most common:

Double-tonguing: This is a way of playing fast notes, and players often do it by quickly mouthing "T-K-T-K" down the instrument. They can go even faster, by *triple*-tonguing! For this they mouth "T-T-K-T-T-K" down the instrument.

Flutter-tonguing: Brass instruments can't do this as well as the flute, but they can make a *kind* of fluttering sound. The player rolls an "R" down the instrument or growls into it.

Vibrato: This is where the note is made to wobble a tiny bit, so the sound is a bit richer. How much it's used depends on the instrument, the player's style and the music being played.

Glissando: A sliding effect up or down. Best on the trombone!

Also, with the right mute in the bell, trumpets can make a "waa-waa" kind of sound. It's amusing, but not very musical.

It's a fact...

The "**water key**" on brass instruments is sometimes called a "spit valve." But it lets out condensation, not spit! Condensation builds up because you breathe warm air down a cold metal tube. When the instrument starts to sound all gurgly, you know it's time to press it...

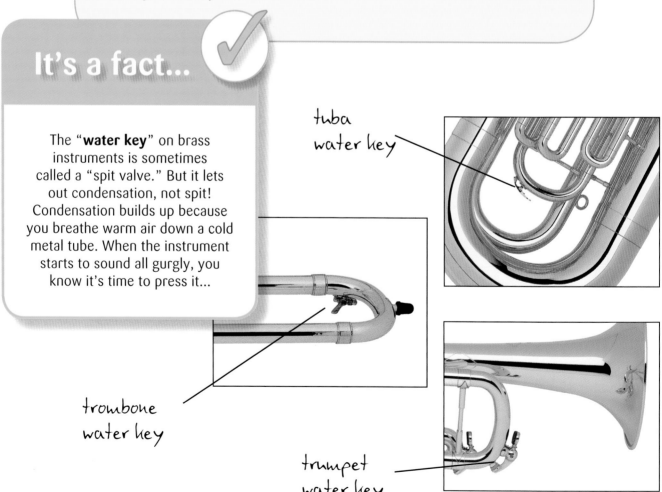

tuba water key

trombone water key

trumpet water key

Brass in the Orchestra

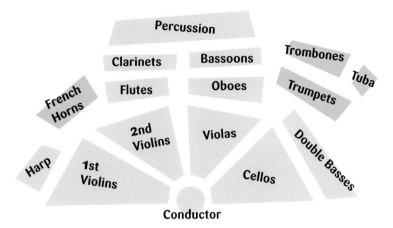

Percussion

Clarinets Bassoons Trombones

Tuba

French Horns Flutes Oboes Trumpets

2nd Violins Violas Double Basses

Harp 1st Violins Cellos

Conductor

The brass section can't be ignored. Not only are the instruments bright and shiny but they make a really impressive sound, especially when they all play together.

In the 18th century, there would usually be just two horns and two trumpets in a brass section. But in the late 19th century, composers like Wagner and Mahler wanted so many brass instruments that there was barely room for them to sit down! The music was *loud*.

These days it's normal to see:

4 or 5 horns
3 trumpets
3 trombones
1 tuba

Playing Together

There's plenty of music for just brass instruments. It can sound magnificent. 400 years ago, an Italian composer called **Giovanni Gabrieli** wrote a lot of it. He made the instruments echo so they sound as if they're all around you.

Outside the orchestra, brass instruments are also found in **brass bands**. Some members - like the cornet and the euphonium - are more at home here than in an orchestra. You might imagine these bands to be deafening, but they can sound surprisingly soft, gentle and relaxing. Of course, when they really go for it and blast with all their strength, the effect is powerful and exciting.

CD-ROM ▶

Hear a Gabrieli Sample Click Sound under "Brass"

> **Brass bands are all very well in their place - outdoors and several miles away.**
>
> Sir Thomas Beecham

The French horn blends particularly well with the woodwind instruments. It's often considered a woodwind instrument by conductors and is placed near the woodwind section.

The Trumpet

Bold as Brass

bell

piston valve

lead pipe

finger ring

cup-shaped
mouthpiece

A silver trumpet was
found in Tutankhamun's tomb in
Egypt in 1922: it had been lying there
undiscovered for 3,000 years. In 1939 a
recording of its sound was made in Cairo for
the BBC - but the strain of being played
made it shatter into pieces!

> The nerves are a
> problem on trumpet,
> because when you
> mess up everyone
> can hear it.
>
> Wynton Marsalis,
> famous trumpeter

Overall

The trumpet is a bold, bright, confident instrument.
It speaks plainly, clearly and often very loudly!

You might hear it playing high, soaring proudly over the top of the
orchestra like a beautiful bird of prey and attracting attention to itself.
It stands out from the crowd and makes sure that you're listening to it.

water key

Trumpets in the Orchestra

Percussion

Clarinets   Bassoons   Trombones

Flutes   Oboes   Tuba

French Horns   Trumpets

2nd Violins   Violas

Harp   1st Violins   Cellos   Double Basses

Conductor

The trumpet often has sudden, loud statements. It loves to come blasting
in with lots of exciting notes and then shut up, leaving you wondering
where it's gone. It's good at fanfares – and so it should be, since those are
all it ever used to play!

Trumpet players have a lot of rests. In some 18th-century music – including
pieces by Haydn, Mozart, Beethoven and Schubert – they spend more time
twiddling their thumbs with nothing to do than actually playing.

But at the end of the 19th century, composers started going crazy. They
wanted more and more brass, so instead of two trumpets you could
find five or six in one piece. Think about how loud *one* trumpet is... then
imagine how loud *six* would be!

Today you will often find three trumpets in the brass section.

When Mozart was little, he was terrified of the trumpet!

You can find trumpets in:

Concertos: Many in the late Baroque and Classical periods. Haydn's Trumpet Concerto (1796) is very famous.

Jazz: The trumpet loves jazz! It can be soulful as well as energetic. Louis Armstrong was a famous jazz trumpeter who did amazing things on the instrument.

Chamber music: Not found here very often – it's a bit too self-important to blend easily with others!

Did you know?

Many years ago, the trumpet became linked with war. It was smart, impressive, strong, loud: all the things that a military instrument should be. Its shape was straight and simple: no holes, valves or keys; no bends or twists – just a plain brass tube.

King Henry VIII and Queen Elizabeth I of England both employed 12 or more trumpeters to be at their beck and call.

Construction of the Trumpet

The trumpet is a cylindrical tube of brass, looped around. It widens to a bell at one end and has a cup-shaped mouthpiece at the other end.

It has three piston valves: The player presses these for different notes.

For more about how valves work, look at page 89.

How do you play it?

1 You put your lips on this:

Of course, it's not quite *that* easy. You need a lot of energy to play the trumpet, especially for long notes. The lips aren't rammed hard onto the mouthpiece, but they have to be fairly firm so that when you press the valves the trumpet doesn't fall off your mouth!

Trumpeters use three things to play different notes:

1) Lips
2) Diaphragm
3) Valves

2 The air that you blow travels through this:

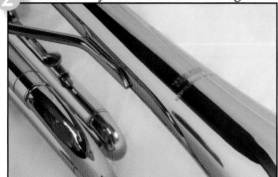

Highs & Lows pitch range

3 You press these:

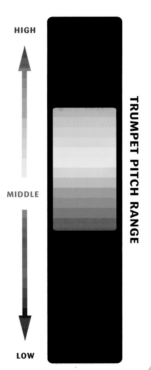

HIGH

MIDDLE

LOW

TRUMPET PITCH RANGE

The trumpet's strong sound can easily overpower other instruments. The trumpet itself is very happy about that, but composers have to be careful how they write for it in the orchestra.

4 And the sound comes blasting out of this:

The quality of playing is actually affected by the spaces in a player's head, throat and chest. When the player blows, these spaces act as "resonators" and affect the sound.

Other Trumpets

Piccolo trumpet

Cornet

Trumpet in B flat

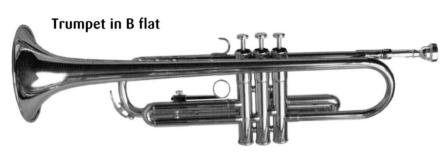
Trumpet in D

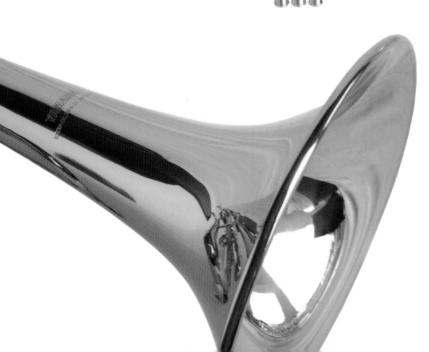

Did you know?

When played together, trumpets and drums can sound quite scary. In wars, they'd encourage the soldiers and frighten the enemy.

There are several kinds of trumpet. It used to come in even more sizes, but these are now the most common:

Trumpet in B flat (the usual one)
Trumpet in C
Trumpet in D / E flat

It's a fact...

J.S. Bach (1685–1750) loved writing really high trumpet parts, which were played on a special, smaller trumpet. In fact, people talk about the "Bach trumpet," but nobody is sure exactly what this instrument was. Today, these high parts are usually played on the piccolo trumpet.

Piccolo trumpet

The piccolo trumpet is the very little one. It has four valves and is happiest playing up high. It's used for a lot of Bach's high trumpet parts today.

Cornet

The cornet looks like a fat trumpet. But its shape gives it a sweeter, less piercing sound.

It's happiest in brass bands, and though it occasionally appears in the orchestra (Rossini's *William Tell* Overture, for example) it doesn't really belong there.

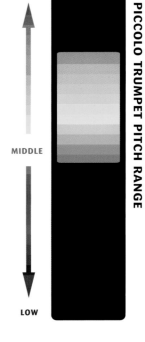

Highs & Lows pitch range

HIGH

MIDDLE

LOW

PICCOLO TRUMPET PITCH RANGE

CD-ROM ▶

Hear the instruments! Click Trumpet Sound under "Brass"

Aida trumpet

There's even an "Aida" trumpet – a very long, straight, thin instrument with one valve. It was designed in the 19th century for **Verdi**'s opera *Aida*... and hasn't been seen since.

The Trombone

Sliding Every Which Way

bell

slide brace

mouthpiece
brace

cup-shaped
mouthpiece

Beethoven was the first
to use trombones in
a symphony. He used them in
his Fifth (1804).

Are you producing as
much sound as possible
from that quaint and
antique drainage system
which you are applying
to your face?

Sir Thomas Beecham, conductor,
talking to a trombonist

Overall

You can spot a trombone a mile off by its long slide. Instead of keys or valves, the trombone has this enormous U-bend that gives the player's right arm a real workout. It's powerful and can blare with the best of them: you don't argue with a trombone.

It can have quite a dark sound – as if something bad is about to happen. Mozart obviously thought so. In his opera *Don Giovanni*, that's exactly when he uses it.

water key

But how could it possibly have a slide like that and not have a funny side? It can sound quite comical – even rude. And the players ("trombonists") don't take themselves too seriously, either!

outer tube
of slide

Trombones in the Orchestra

Trombones sound lower than trumpets but higher than tubas.

Percussion

Clarinets   Bassoons   Trombones

French Horns   Flutes   Oboes   Trumpets   Tuba

2nd Violins   Violas   Double Basses

Harp   1st Violins   Cellos

Conductor

Today, you often find three trombones in an orchestra: two "tenor" trombones and a "bass" trombone.

You don't hear one trombone on its own very often. The best trombone effect is when they all play together: they're strong and magnificent. To see their gleaming slides all being pushed and pulled at exactly the same time adds to the excitement of the music.

Trombones work well in groups. The great composer Berlioz said: "A single trombone seems out of place. The instrument needs harmony..."

It's a fact...

A composer called Jan Sandström wrote a piece called "Motorbike" Concerto for the famous trombonist Christian Lindberg. The soloist is the hero, who travels the world on a Harley Davidson motorbike. Lindberg wore a leather jacket on stage when he first performed the concerto!

The English composers **Edward Elgar** and **Gustav Holst** were both trombonists.

Construction of the Trombone

The trombone is a long brass tube. It widens to a bell at one end and has a cup-shaped mouthpiece at the other end. Part of the tube slides in and out, which is how the trombone can sound all its notes.

This **slide** was a very clever idea – it meant that the trombone was able to play a full range of notes long before any other brass instrument.

Trombones often play in:

Jazz: In the 1930s and 1940s, jazz bands – called "big bands" – often had four trombones.

Concertos: A few, from very early to the present day.

Brass bands: It likes to have fun with the family.

How do you play it?

- Hold the trombone almost horizontally out in front of you.
- Press your lips to the mouthpiece.
- Take a deep breath, and blow.
- Move the slide in and out for different notes.

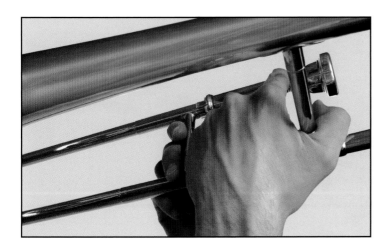

As with all other brass instruments, you need good support from your diaphragm muscle to control your breath. And although it sounds funny, the big challenge is co-ordinating your slide with your tongue!

The slide takes skill and practice to use. It can extend almost a yard, but it has to be within a quarter-inch to hit each note accurately. And that has to happen as quickly as a trumpet player can press a valve! Suddenly the trombone doesn't seem quite so easy...

Did you know?

In about 1500, the early trombone – the sackbut – had a slide and could play many different notes. 300 years later, valves were invented for the other brass instruments. The trombone didn't need valves, it already had a slide!

Special Effects

Glissando is like a big swoop up or down. Because the trombone can go smoothly from one note to the next with its slide, it's a natural!

It's a fact...

The early trombone was called a "**sackbut**." The name came from the French word "saqueboute," meaning "push-pull." That's what you do with the slide!

Highs & Lows pitch range

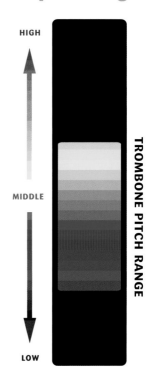

HIGH

MIDDLE

LOW

TROMBONE PITCH RANGE

Other Trombones

Numbers have shrunk a bit since the trombone's early days. There used to be different-sized versions that played together as a group. Now, there's the normal one – called the "tenor" trombone – plus:

Bass trombone
(Used to be called the "tenor-bass" trombone)

This sounds even lower than the tenor trombone, with more tubing.

Alto trombone

This one is smaller than the tenor trombone, but you don't see it very often!

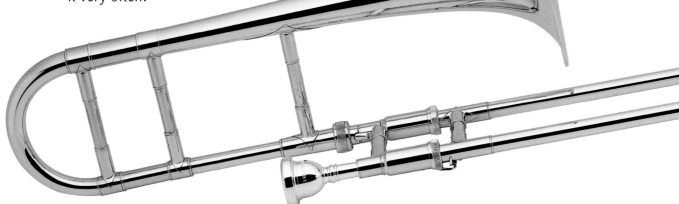

 CD-ROM ▶

Hear the instruments! Click Trombone Sound under "Brass"

Did you know ?

If you stretched out the tubing of a trombone, it would be nearly nine feet long: further than the floor to the ceiling!

There used to be a contrabass trombone. But when you hear that one trombonist called it a "tank," you can imagine why it's out of a job these days.

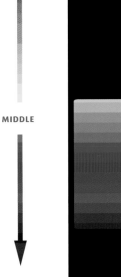

Highs & Lows pitch range

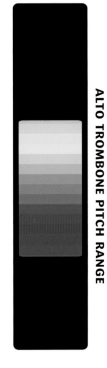

HIGH

MIDDLE

LOW

BASS TROMBONE PITCH RANGE

ALTO TROMBONE PITCH RANGE

The French Horn
Spaghetti Spiral of the Brass

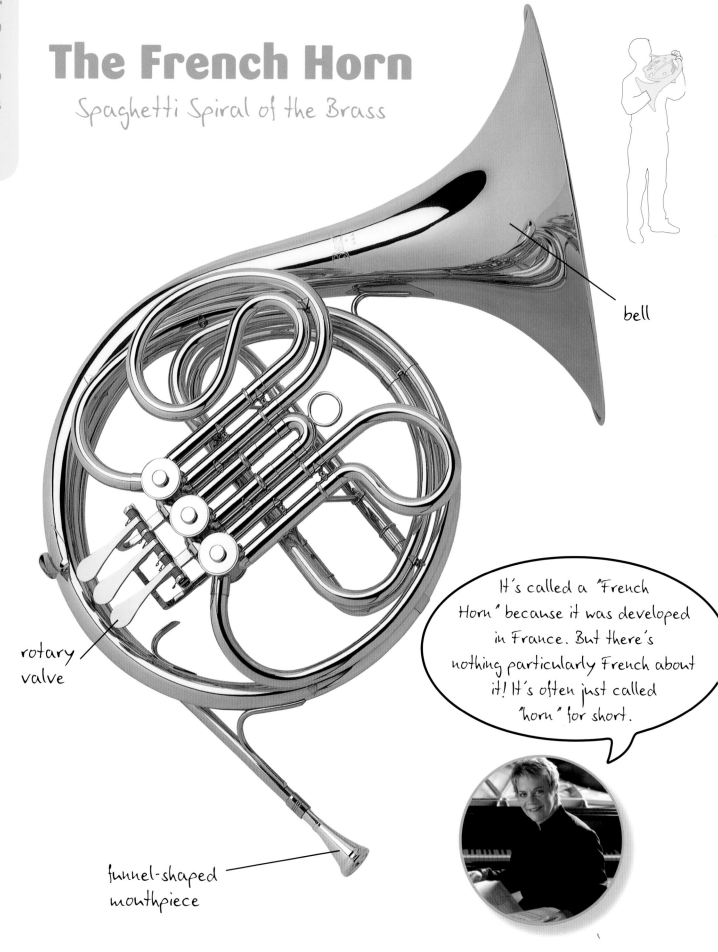

bell

rotary valve

funnel-shaped mouthpiece

It's called a "French Horn" because it was developed in France. But there's nothing particularly French about it! It's often just called "horn" for short.

Overall

The French horn is probably the most difficult instrument to play – even more difficult than the violin. The most expert players can still fluff the occasional note. But its smooth, velvety sound is a world away from the rest of the brass section.

It produces two main sounds:
1) Soft, golden, velvety
2) Loud, extrovert, rousing

French Horns in the Orchestra

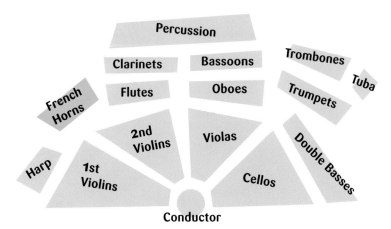

There are normally four horns in the orchestra, though there can be eight. Sometimes they play in pairs, with one playing the higher notes and one doing the lower notes.

The sound of the horns is typical of the Romantic era. This was in the 19th century, when composers like Schumann, Wagner, Brahms and Bruckner wanted huge, rich sounds. Their music often depicts outdoor scenes.

Horns get big, beefy solos. They're good at swelling the sound of the orchestra, as well as playing long, held notes in the background.

Horns sound like a cross between the brass instruments and the woodwind. Although they *are* brass instruments, their sound can be very gentle. They blend much better with the woodwind than do the trumpet, trombone or tuba.

It's a fact...

Hundreds of years ago, the horn's place was in the hunt. Horsemen would carry it and use it to sound signals. That's why it has a round, coiled shape – so that it could fit over the horseman's shoulder when it wasn't being played. He was free to take up the reins and gallop at full speed...

Did you know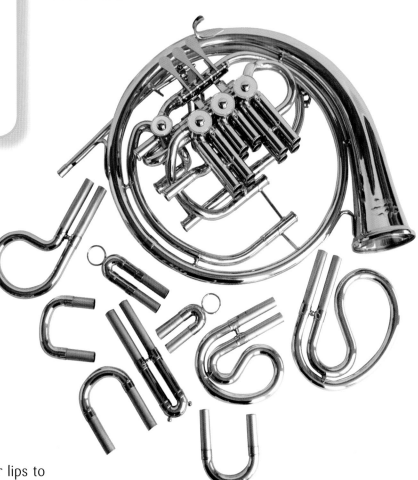

Mozart wrote his horn concertos for his friend Joseph Leutgeb. When he wrote the notes, he used lots of colored inks to put Leutgeb off. And there were little insults and comments through the music – like "Bet you can't play this!"

Construction of the Horn

The horn is made of brass. It's curled around to form a neat circle and ends in a wide bell.

Unlike the other brass instruments, it has a mouthpiece shaped like a funnel. (See p. 104)

There are three rotary valves for different notes. (See p. 104)

How do you play it?

Like other brass instruments, you put your lips to the mouthpiece and "blow a raspberry."

The vibration of your lips sends vibrating waves of air whizzing through all those little bits of tube.

The valves can redirect the air so that different notes can be sounded.

But the horn is really difficult! Sometimes the notes can "split": really, that's just what it sounds like.

You can hear a horn in:

Concertos and Solos: Mozart wrote four famous concertos; Richard Strauss two. There are some solos for horn and piano, but not many.

Chamber music: Many wind quintets (with flute, oboe, clarinet, bassoon), as the horn blends well with the woodwinds.

Horn players put one hand up the bell of their instrument when they play. They do it to make tiny adjustments to the sound. They can even make the pitch "bend" - so it slides up and down a tiny bit. It's called "portamento." Britten used this effect in his Serenade for tenor, horn and strings.

Other Horns

There are two other types of horns, including one odd relation.

Wagner tuba

It's shaped like a tuba, but it has a mouthpiece like that of a horn. So it's usually horn players who have to play it. It was invented by Wagner in the 1860s. Wagner liked to do things his own way. His cycle of four operas, called *The Ring of the Nibelung*, involves a fantastical, heavenly palace called Valhalla. Wagner decided that this place was so extraordinary it needed a whole new instrument to conjure up its atmosphere. So he invented the Wagner tuba.

Did you know

In London's Albert Hall in 1956, the famous horn player Dennis Brain performed Leopold Mozart's Alpine Horn Concerto on a garden hose!

Double horn

In about 1900, the double horn was invented. It's like two-horns-in-one. The basic French horn is in F, but there's a higher one in B flat. The double horn puts the two together. It took a long time to catch on, but many players now use it.

On the double horn there's a thumb trigger for switching between the F part and the B flat part. It makes sure the air is diverted into different bits of tubing.

For more about how valves work, look at page 89.

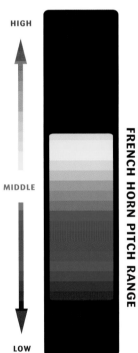

Highs & Lows pitch range

HIGH

MIDDLE

LOW

FRENCH HORN PITCH RANGE

The double horn can go even higher.

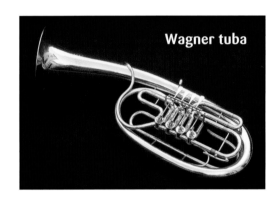

Wagner tuba

An ancestor of the horn was called a "**serpent**." It looked like its name! When the composer Handel first heard one he cried "What the devil is that?"

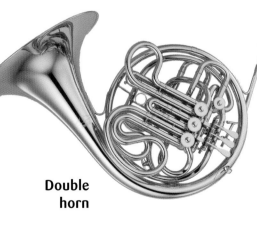

Double horn

CD-ROM ▶

Hear the instruments! Click French Horn Sound under "Brass"

The Tuba

Gentle Giant

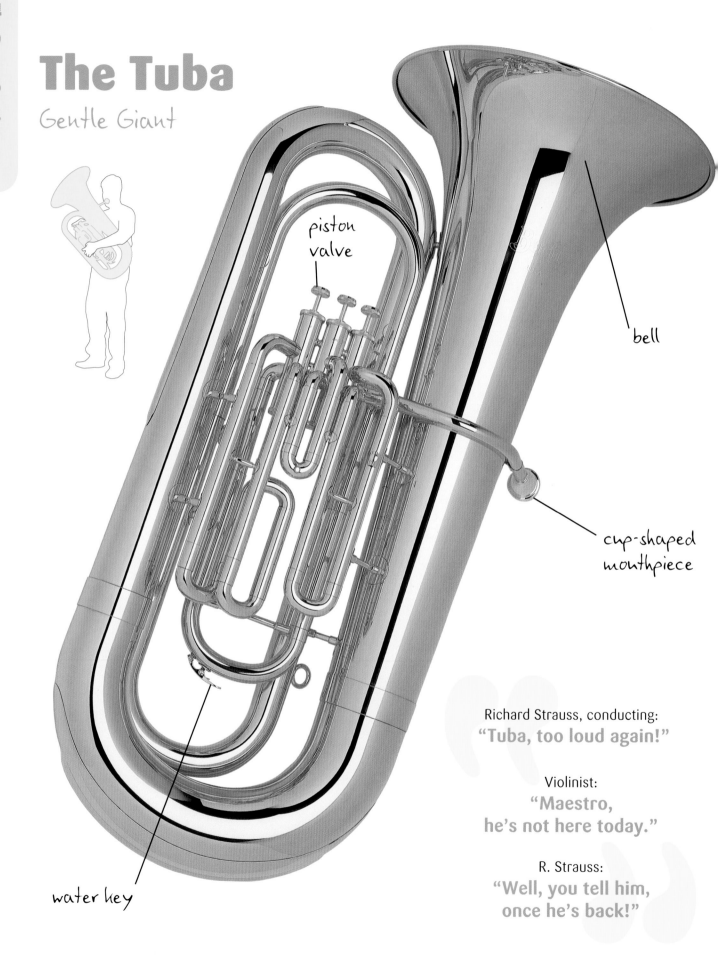

piston valve

bell

cup-shaped mouthpiece

water key

Richard Strauss, conducting:
"Tuba, too loud again!"

Violinist:
**"Maestro,
he's not here today."**

R. Strauss:
**"Well, you tell him,
once he's back!"**

Overall

"Oom-pah, oom-pah" isn't *all* the tuba can do. Sadly, that is what it's famous for! It's the biggest and lowest brass instrument. It's so big, you can hardly see the player behind it.

Looking at it, you'd think it played nothing but slow notes. But it can be amazingly light and agile, running around with fast notes like the smaller brass instruments.

It can also make a round, rich, mellow sound. The English composer Vaughan Williams knew that: his Tuba Concerto gives the instrument a rare opportunity to enjoy the limelight.

Did you know

Famous entertainer and cartoonist **Gerard Hoffnung** was a tuba player. He once remarked that when he was practicing the tuba, the neighbors thought he had an elephant stuck in his bathroom.

CD-ROM ▶

Hear Vaughan Williams' Tuba Concerto Click Tuba Sound under "Brass"

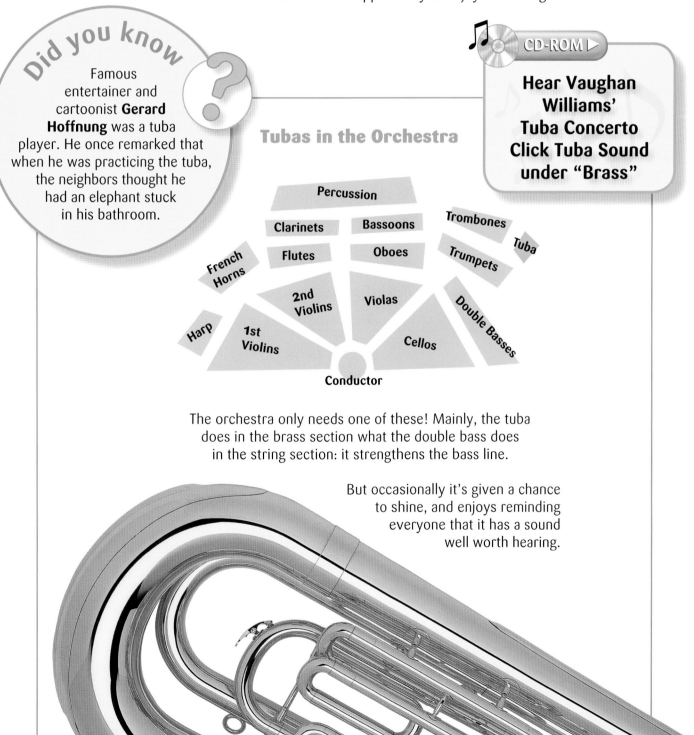

Tubas in the Orchestra

Percussion

Clarinets · Bassoons · Trombones · Tuba

French Horns · Flutes · Oboes · Trumpets

2nd Violins · Violas · Double Basses

Harp · 1st Violins · Cellos

Conductor

The orchestra only needs one of these! Mainly, the tuba does in the brass section what the double bass does in the string section: it strengthens the bass line.

But occasionally it's given a chance to shine, and enjoys reminding everyone that it has a sound well worth hearing.

Tubas play in:

Brass bands: The tuba is quite at home here! The tenor version, called a "euphonium," spends almost all its time in brass bands.

Concertos: A famous one by Vaughan Williams, but not many others.

In Wagner's opera *Siegfried*, the tuba plays the dragon's music.

The tuba's tubes are so complicated that it was once described as a "plumber's nightmare"!

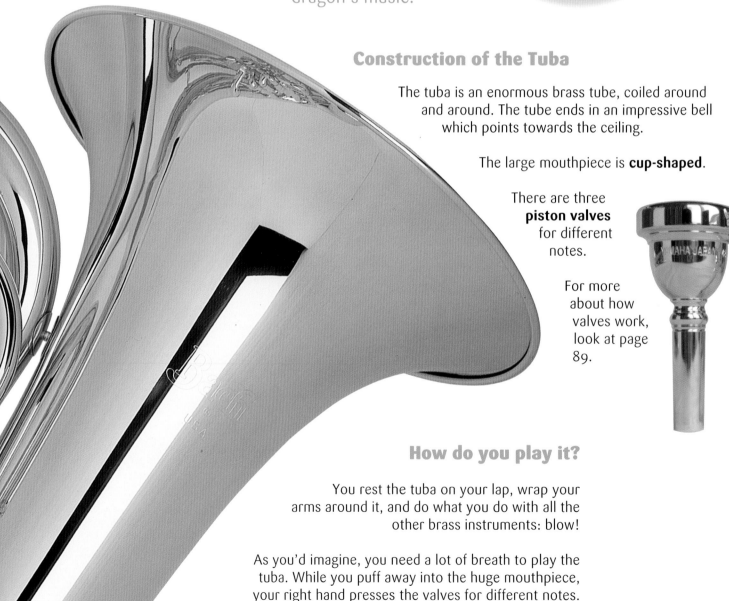

Construction of the Tuba

The tuba is an enormous brass tube, coiled around and around. The tube ends in an impressive bell which points towards the ceiling.

The large mouthpiece is **cup-shaped**.

There are three **piston valves** for different notes.

For more about how valves work, look at page 89.

How do you play it?

You rest the tuba on your lap, wrap your arms around it, and do what you do with all the other brass instruments: blow!

As you'd imagine, you need a lot of breath to play the tuba. While you puff away into the huge mouthpiece, your right hand presses the valves for different notes.

Other Tubas

The tuba we see all the time in the orchestra is the bass tuba.
But there are other versions.

Euphonium

It's a fact...

Before the tuba, there was a similar instrument with the weird name of "**ophicleide**." But it wasn't only hard to say – it was hard to play! A few 19th-century composers wrote for the ophicleide but they switched when the tuba was invented in 1835.

Euphonium
(tenor tuba)

"**Euphonium**" means "**well-sounding**" in Greek. It has a rare solo in "Mars" of Holst's *Planets*, but otherwise it sticks to brass bands.

Contrabass tuba

This is lower than the bass tuba – so just imagine how big it is! It's very rare to see one...

CD-ROM ▷

Hear the instruments! Click Tuba Sound under "Brass"

Family Highs & Lows - Pitch Ranges Together

Below, you can see how the brass family fits together, from top to bottom.

HIGH

MIDDLE

LOW

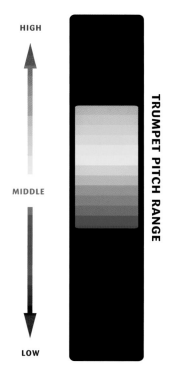

TRUMPET PITCH RANGE

TROMBONE PITCH RANGE

FRENCH HORN PITCH RANGE

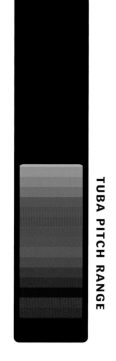

TUBA PITCH RANGE

THE PERCUSSION
The Colorful Clatterers

It's a fact...

The oldest percussion instrument is a pair of **hands**: babies can clap before they can speak, and have probably been doing it since time began.

Overall

The percussion family, otherwise known as the "kitchen department" of the orchestra, includes anything that can be struck, shaken, rubbed, knocked, scratched, slapped or stroked to make a sound.

There are so many instruments, from so many cultures and backgrounds, that it would be impossible for one percussionist to cover them all in his or her lifetime.

The 20th century was when percussion really took off: composers like Stravinsky, Varèse, Cage, Bartók, Messiaen and Boulez showed just how much could be done with a percussion section. It was used much more cleverly: it didn't just bang and crash anymore. And the range of instruments expanded, with traditional instruments from Africa, Latin America and the Far East (gongs, cymbals, drums and xylophones) joining in.

Solo percussionists emerged.

Evelyn Glennie has made an extremely successful career as a solo percussionist, despite being profoundly deaf. In fact, her deafness doesn't bother her at all – she can *feel* **vibrations**: the low ones in her legs and feet, and the high ones sometimes in particular places on her face, neck and chest.

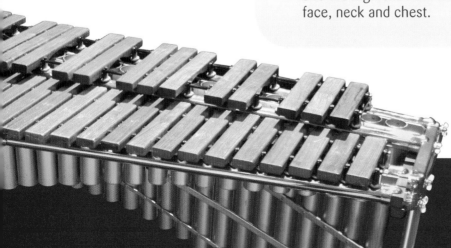

Percussion in the Orchestra

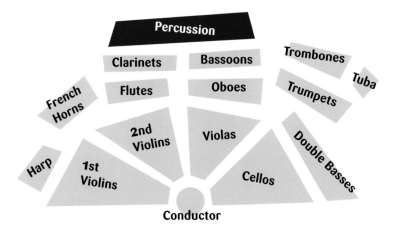

The percussion section is the most exotic part of the orchestra, and has the greatest variety of sound. Instruments come from all over the world.

A composer *can* include anything at all in a piece, so if you're a percussionist you might be asked to do all kinds of things, such as tap on a typewriter, pop a cork, or even fire a pistol. Percussionists don't just know how to play *one* of the percussion instruments: they are multi-talented and can play many instruments!

The variety makes it a colorful section. It can do almost anything, from gentle tunes or little chimes, to massive, exciting bangs and crashes. Composers can ask for all sorts of weird and wonderful sounds to go with the other orchestral instruments. They might be something like this...

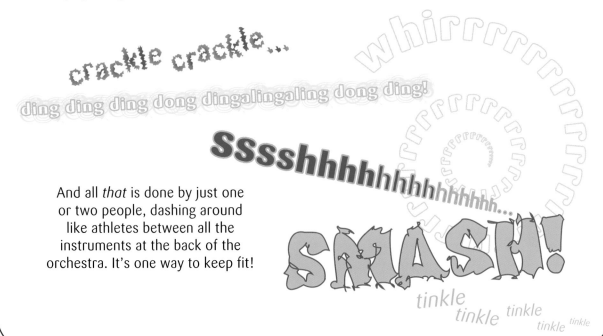

And all *that* is done by just one or two people, dashing around like athletes between all the instruments at the back of the orchestra. It's one way to keep fit!

The Percussionist

Playing percussion isn't easy. Here are some of the skills you need:

- **Co-ordination:** Unlike everyone else in the orchestra, you often have to play several things at once with both hands and feet. If you can't pat your head and rub your stomach at the same time, you might not make a good percussionist!

- **Sense of rhythm:** Percussionists must be rhythmic and precise. Imagine walloping a bass drum or clashing a cymbal at the wrong moment!

- **Confidence:** You're on your own at the back of the orchestra with some of the loudest instruments. You just have to believe in yourself and go for it.

- **Musicality:** All orchestral players need this. It means being sensitive towards the music they are playing: they have to listen, and know how to blend in with everyone. You might think that percussionists, because they "just hit things," don't need to be "musical" at all. But this isn't true. Striking a drum, for example, can be done in many different ways: it needs judgment and a good ear to know exactly how hard and at what angle to bring down the beater onto the instrument. The sense of *touch* is really important.

Did you know

Percussionists often don't own all the instruments, as there are so many to play! But they always have their own set of sticks, hammers, mallets or beaters.

It's a fact...

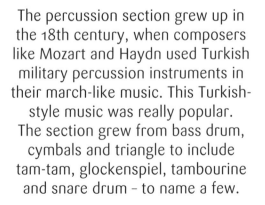

The percussion section grew up in the 18th century, when composers like Mozart and Haydn used Turkish military percussion instruments in their march-like music. This Turkish-style music was really popular. The section grew from bass drum, cymbals and triangle to include tam-tam, glockenspiel, tambourine and snare drum – to name a few.

Eugene Ormandy is conductor of the Philadelphia Orchestra in the USA. This was a conversation between him and the percussion section in one rehearsal:

Ormandy: **"Percussion a little louder."**
Percussion: **"We don't have anything."**
Ormandy: **"That's right, play it louder."**

Apparently he wasn't listening!

What is in the percussion section?

In theory, percussion could include anything that makes a sound
(just think what you have in your kitchen cupboards...). Seeing as the French
composer Erik Satie asked for a typewriter in his *Parade*, perhaps the next
composer will want a fly swatter, or maybe a lawnmower...

In reality, there are two groups of percussion instruments that are
used in many pieces:

1) Tuned Percussion
(percussion of "definite pitch")

These instruments can produce more than
one note, or pitch. The most common are:

Timpani (or "Kettledrums") – the only
drums that can produce different pitches
Xylophone
Marimba
Glockenspiel
Vibraphone
Tubular Bells (or "Chimes")
Celesta (or "Celeste")

2) Untuned Percussion
(percussion of "indefinite pitch")

These instruments don't have a definite pitch:
they just produce one sound. The most common
are:

Snare drum (or "Side drum")   Wood block
Bass drum   Cymbals
Tom-tom   Castanets
Bongos   Maracas
Tambourine   Tam-tam
Triangle

Beaters

The instrument is one thing, but the stick used to strike it is another. Sometimes, as with the tambourine, your hands do all the work. But many other instruments need beaters, and percussionists have whole cases full of different kinds: very soft to very hard; very light to very heavy; very small to very big.

The beaters come in all kinds of colors, too, indicating their weight and strength. So whether you use red with stripes, blue without stripes, or yellow with a cushion may actually mean a difference in sound. It's not just for fun!

It's a fact...

The radical 20th-century Hungarian composer György Ligeti wrote a piece called *Aventure* which asks one percussionist for many weird things, including:

"...paper bags (to pop)... toy frog (to squeak); balloons (to squeak); cloth (to tear); book (to flick pages); tin foil (to rustle); empty suitcase (to hit); metal trash can and tray of dishes (dishes to be thrown into trash)..."

– and the list goes on!

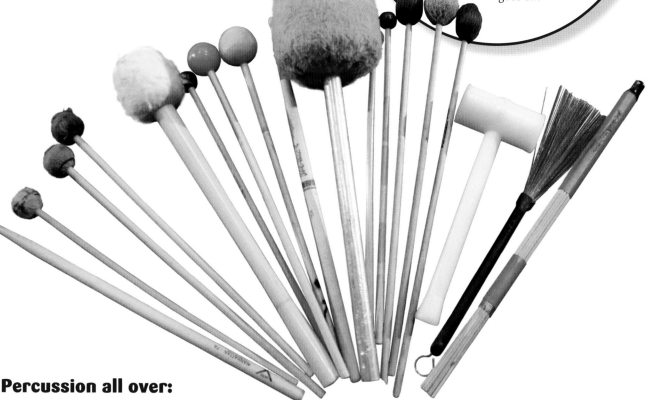

Percussion all over:

Concertos: There are timpani concertos from the Baroque era (1600–1750) but most others have been written since the mid-1980s. Since the percussionist has to play lots of instruments, it's almost like an obstacle course as much as a musical performance! The effect is exciting to hear *and* to see.

Solo pieces: There are pieces for all sorts of instruments and combinations of instruments. The repertoire is growing all the time.

Jazz: Drums belong here, of course! So does the vibraphone.

Pop music: Pop music would be lost without percussion: nearly all of it has a drumbeat.

World music: Percussion instruments aren't just *used* in music from around the world – they've *come* from around the world. That's why the percussion section is so exotic and colorful.

Tuned Percussion

These are the ones that can play different pitches, or notes.

Timpani
(or "Kettledrums")

"Timpani" is plural. The singular is "timpano," but nobody ever says "timpano"! People always talk about "timpani" as a group - or they say "kettledrums"...

Timpani pedal

All drums are called "**membranophones**." The word "membrane" means a thin layer of skin. Drums have a thin layer of skin, or material pretending to be skin, stretched across the top.

Did you know

Some orchestras feature a "**timpanist**" who does not play any other percussion instrument. It's because timpani feature so much in orchestral music – timpanists don't have time to go running around tinkling a triangle or rattling a tambourine as *well*! They're quite busy enough with just their drums.

Timpani Construction

Timpani are ancient: a cave-man who banged on an animal skin stretched over a wooden or bone frame wasn't so different from a timpani player of today!

The drum has a copper bowl, a bit like a huge tea-cup. Across the top of it there's a flat, smooth surface (or "head") of plastic, fiberskin or calfskin. A plastic head is more reliable, because it doesn't change when it gets hot or cold, or damp or dry, like skin does. And it doesn't break as easily.

At the bottom of modern timpani is a foot-pedal. A timpanist uses this pedal to tune the drum before the rehearsal or concert begins. Tuning one of these drums is really difficult. You need a "good ear" and lots of patience. The pedal can also make the drum do a brilliant "glissando." As you strike the drum, the pitch of the note slides up or down.

How do you play them?

You strike them with sticks or beaters. Different kinds make different sounds, and players are experts at knowing which are best in which piece.

It's also important where the beater falls on the wide timpani head. Near the edge produces a clearer pitch than in the middle, which is more like a thud.

You need to be able to count, too. Like other percussionists, timpanists have a lot of rests, when they don't play at all. But if they fall asleep, or think about what they had for breakfast, that's it: they're lost. They have to follow the music and count all the time. When you have an instrument that makes a loud boom, you don't want to come bursting in at the wrong time!

It's a fact...

"Trumpets and drums" often means trumpets and timpani. Their combined strong sounds have been very useful in war; and since the 17th century, composers have used them together to celebrate the glory of God.

What sound do they make?

Boom!

Timpani are "tuned." The idea of drums sounding different pitches, or notes, might seem strange – but they can. Each drum has a range of at least five whole notes.

There might be four timpani in the orchestra, all different sizes, pounding on their own notes. They usually play in short bursts, and often add power to the orchestra's sound.

They can sound very exciting. Beethoven knew that: he was the first to give them a proper solo, at the beginning of his Violin Concerto.

They can even create particular effects, such as a heartbeat or gunfire. They're good at it: that's why they became top of the percussion section.

Remember, remember

If a drum skin is **slack**, the sound is **low**.

If a drum skin is **tight**, the sound is **high**.

Hector Berlioz, the 19th-century French composer who liked big sounds, asked for 16 timpani in his Requiem! A Requiem is written in memory of a dead person, or people. With 16 timpani, you'd think he was trying to wake them up again...

CD-ROM ▶

Hear the instruments! Click Timpani Sound under "Percussion"

Highs & Lows pitch range

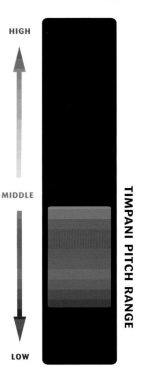

HIGH

MIDDLE

LOW

TIMPANI PITCH RANGE

A whole set of timpani can cover this range.

Xylophone

In Greek, "xylo" means "**wood**" and "phone" means "**sound**" – hence "wood sound."

Xylophone Construction

A xylophone has two rows of wooden bars, laid out like a piano keyboard. They are in order of length, like the piano's strings: the shorter ones sound higher notes and the longer ones sound lower notes.

Under each bar is a short, metal pipe (or "resonator") running downwards. This helps the sound when the bar is struck: it resonates.

How do you play it?

You stand over it and strike the wooden bars with beaters, usually made of wood, plastic, rubber or latex.

Highs & Lows pitch range

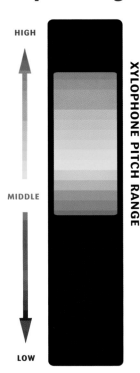

XYLOPHONE PITCH RANGE

HIGH

MIDDLE

LOW

Camille Saint-Saëns used the xylophone in his *Danse Macabre* to sound like the rattling of bones!

What sound does it make?

The beaters on the wooden bars make a dry, choppy sound. It's heard a lot in music from around the world. In Africa, xylophones used to be made out of simple logs.

When you strike a bar, the note doesn't last long (if you keep your stick on the bar, it makes no difference). So to make the sound last a bit longer, players might "roll" (alternate the sticks one after the other at a rapid speed on one or more bars).

Different beaters can make the sound softer and mellower, or louder and harsher.

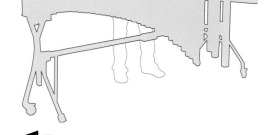

CD-ROM ▶

Hear the instruments! Click Xylophone Sound under "Percussion"

Marimba

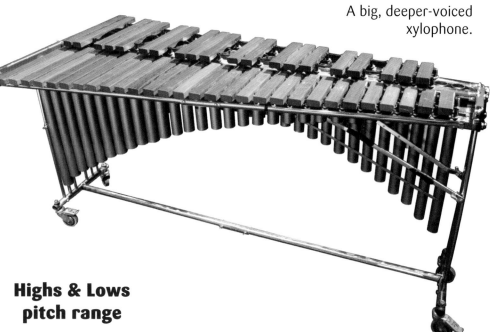

What is it?

A big, deeper-voiced xylophone.

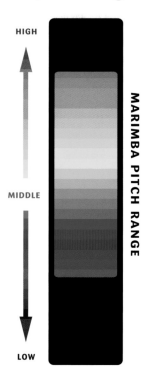

HIGH

MIDDLE

LOW

MARIMBA PITCH RANGE

Highs & Lows
pitch range

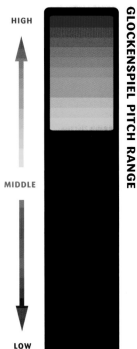

HIGH

MIDDLE

LOW

GLOCKENSPIEL PITCH RANGE

Glockenspiel

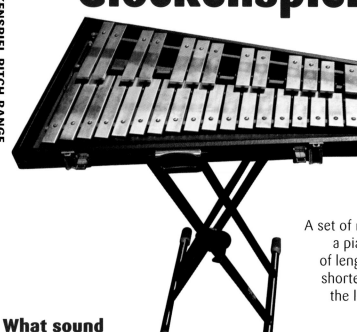

"Glockenspiel" means "**bell-play**" in German.

What is it?

A set of metal (steel) bars arranged like a piano keyboard. They sit in order of length, like the piano's strings: the shorter ones sound higher notes and the longer ones sound lower notes.

What sound does it make?

It makes a tinkling, bright, cheerful sound.

How do you play it?

You stand over it and strike the bars with beaters, usually made of plastic or brass.

Vibraphone

What is it?

A fancy glockenspiel!

The vibraphone (called "vibes" for short) was invented in America. It was first used in jazz and pop music in the 1920s, but soon caught on in orchestras.

It has a set of metal bars arranged from longest (lowest) to shortest (highest).

Underneath each bar is a tube (or resonator) to help project the sound – as with the xylophone. But that's not all: on top of each tube is a little disc. The disc is spun around by an electric motor so that when you strike the bar, the sound vibrates and quivers a bit.

The vibraphone even has a "sustain" pedal, which means you can make the notes last longer.

The vibraphone is so called because it makes a throbbing, "**vibrating**" sound.

Vibraphone discs

Highs & Lows pitch range

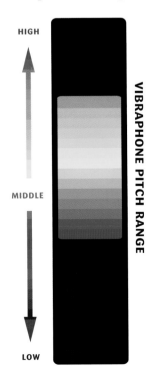

HIGH

MIDDLE

LOW

VIBRAPHONE PITCH RANGE

How do you play it?

You strike the bars with beaters, usually made of rubber, yarn, wool or latex. The bars can also be bowed using a violin or cello bow.

What sound does it make?

It has a metallic sound but it can be quite soothing, due to the vibrato (vibrating sound). Its sound isn't crisp like the xylophone's: it's as if the edges have been rounded off, making it warmer and more relaxed.

CD-ROM ▶

Hear the instruments! Click Glockenspiel, Marimba, or Vibraphone Sound under "Percussion"

Tubular Bells
(or "Chimes")

What are they?

A row of metal tubes hung in order of length (in two rows) from a horizontal frame. The shorter ones sound higher notes; the longer ones sound lower notes.

If you line up drinking glasses of different sizes, and tap them lightly with a spoon, they all produce different notes. The smaller ones are higher and the bigger ones are lower. Try it! It's the same idea with these tubes.

Highs & Lows
pitch range

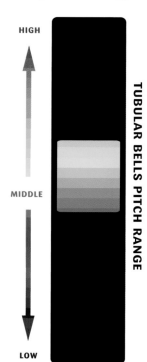

HIGH

MIDDLE

LOW

TUBULAR BELLS PITCH RANGE

How do you play them?

You strike the very top of the chimes with a bell mallet. A pedal can help to sustain or deaden the sound.

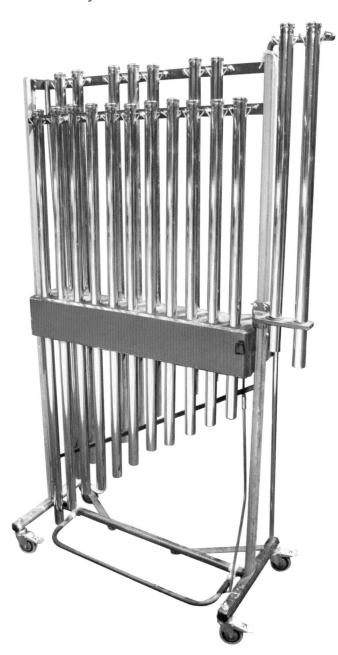

What sound do they make?

The sound of **bells**. Bells have been used for years to ring out at weddings, call people to church, or as a warning of attack. But traditional bells are big and heavy, so in the 1880s tubular bells were invented for the orchestra. They could be taken easily from place to place, but could still imitate the sound of big bells in a belfry.

Composers often use them to sound like church bells.

Celesta
(or "Celeste")

What is it?

It's like a grown-up glockenspiel with a keyboard. It works mechanically, so that when you press keys little felt-covered hammers come up and hit steel bars.

Because the hitting is done mechanically, it's easier than a glockenspiel to play chords – and to play fast!

There's a foot-pedal to control the dampers. These make the steel bars stop vibrating, so the notes don't last as long as they would otherwise.

The celesta is a **keyboard instrument** but it doesn't need tuning like the piano. That's because it doesn't have strings inside.

Highs & Lows pitch range

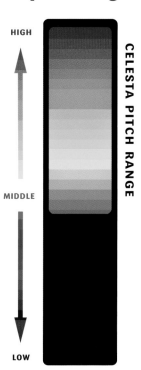

HIGH

MIDDLE

LOW

CELESTA PITCH RANGE

How do you play it?

You play it like a piano: it's usually played by a pianist.

What sound does it make?

Sweet, fairylike tinkling.

CD-ROM ▶

Hear the instruments! Click Tubular Bells or Celesta Sound under "Percussion"

Untuned Percussion

This is the group that can include just about anything at all. Gunshots, typewriters, iron chains... whatever next?!

A few of the most common ones are described here.

It's a fact...

These instruments can create many sound effects but not really pitches, which is why the neutral clef is used when the music is written down:

Snare drum
(or "Side drum")

What is it?

It's a drum with two heads! A shallow cylinder has one head stretched across one end (the "batter" head) and another head stretched across the other end (the "snare" head). The snare head has snares touching it. These are strands of wire, gut or silk that vibrate when you strike the drum.

Snare drums have been around for hundreds of years, in war and in music.

The snare drum is also called a **"side drum"** because in military bands it's slung across the player's shoulder like a satchel and carried to the side.

What sound does it make?

It makes a dry, rattling sound. It can help to build excitement (as it does in Ravel's famous *Boléro*) and it's also good at getting people's attention. Drum rolls are very effective.

How do you play it?

You use two wooden sticks or wire brushes to strike it.

You need a lot of skill to play the snare drum properly. The agility of the hands and fingers is essential for a clean, crisp result.

 CD-ROM ▶

Hear the instruments! Click Snare Drum Sound under "Percussion"

Bass Drum

It's a fact...

The sound of the bass drum is sometimes "felt" more than "heard" because it's so deep and resonant.

What is it?

A very large drum. It's so large that it usually hangs on a metal frame.

It became popular in the 18th century, when there was a craze for music with a Turkish sound.

It often has two heads, like the snare drum. But there are no wires to make the sound rattle.

How do you play it?

You strike it with a large beater. The head of the beater is soft, often covered with felt or wool.

A "**roll**" on a drum is like when you roll an "r", but it's done with beaters instead of your tongue.

What sound does it make?

An enormous, **booming** sound!

It's sometimes used to imitate thunder because of the rumbling noise it can make when it's "rolled," softly.

Tom-tom

What is it?

The tom-tom is a cylindrical drum with no snares attached (unlike the snare drum). It can have either one or two heads. The shell is usually made of wood.

Tom-toms come in varying sizes, from about 6 to 16 inches in diameter. The bigger ones make a lower sound and the smaller ones make a higher sound. They often come in pairs.

In the West, tom-toms can be tuned and can imitate the sounds of, for example, Indian, African and Chinese drums.

How do you play it?

You can play a tom-tom with drum sticks, mallets, bare hands, brushes or a variety of other implements.

What sound does it make?

A satisfying "bom-bom" sound. It can range from low to high and soft to very loud.

CD-ROM ▶

Hear the instruments! Click Bass Drum or Tom-tom Sound under "Percussion"

Bongos

What are they?

Bongos come from Latin America and are an exotic addition to the orchestra. They're joined in pairs, where one is a bit bigger than the other.

The body of each one is wooden, with a skin stretched across the top.

The "conga" is like one big bongo drum, with a longer body.

How do you play them?

They're played either with the hands – tapping out complicated rhythms – or a choice of many different types of sticks, hammers, mallets or beaters.

What sound do they make?

A colorful, high-pitched "bup-bup-bup" sound.

Tambourine

What is it?

The tambourine is a very old instrument, going back as far as 3,000 B.C.

It's a hand-held instrument – a bit like a very shallow drum without a bottom. Around the wooden side, there are small metal discs, which jangle.

What sound does it make?

When it's struck, the surface of the tambourine makes a short, dead sound. But the little discs jangle, whatever you do with it (even when you're trying to keep it quiet!).

How do you play it?

Composers often use it to create the feeling of an exotic dance.

There are many ways to play a tambourine. Three common ways are:

1) You **strike** it with your fingers, hand or fist.
2) You **shake** it.
3) You wet your finger and **drag** it over the surface.

Triangle

What is it?

A metal bar, bent into a triangular shape with a gap in one corner.

What sound does it make?

A tinkling sound. And when you shake the stick backwards and forwards really quickly in the middle of the triangle, it sounds a bit like someone's doorbell.

How do you play it?

You tap it with a little metal stick.

Wood Block

What sound does it make?

A sharp, dry, wood sound.

Did you know?

The triangle might be very small, but you still need to concentrate so you don't go "ding" in the wrong place. And sometimes, when you dangle the triangle from the top, it swings away when you want to hit it and you miss!

What is it?

A small hollow wooden block in the shape of a rectangle. There is a small slit in the edge to increase the sound.

Sometimes there are round-shaped blocks – these are called "**temple blocks**."

Two hollow wooden sticks tapped together are called "**claves**."

How do you play it?

You strike it with a little beater or mallet.

CD-ROM ▶

Hear the instruments! Click Bongos, Tambourine, Triangle, or Wood Block Sound under "Percussion"

Cymbals

What are they?

Cymbals go back thousands of years.
They originated in Turkey and China.

A cymbal is a large disc made of copper mixed with
tin. In the middle of the outside is a little dome, where
there's a strap to hold onto so that you can strike two
cymbals against each other.

Cymbals are often used in pairs, or a single cymbal
can be placed on a
cymbal stand.

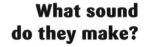

What sound do they make?

An impressive "whoosh" or
"crash" which echoes for a
long time. You can stop the
echo by "dampening" the
cymbals. This means touching
them gently against something
(normally your body). They
echo because they're vibrating
so if you make them still,
the echo stops.

If you strike one cymbal
with a stick, the sound
is less dramatic.

Sometimes, people shuffle
the two cymbals together
to make a mysterious
sort of "sshh" sound.

How do you play them?

You stand with one cymbal in each
hand and bring them together to create
a wonderful whoosh of sound! People
look very important when they play the
cymbals: after a dramatic **"crash,"** they
hold them apart like two trophies.

Crotales

Crotales are tiny cymbals often laid out in a row, in size order. Each sounds a different pitch (the smallest are highest; the largest are lowest), so they are actually "tuned" percussion with a "definite pitch."

They make a light, crisp "ting" when they're struck and a beautiful, magical sound when bowed.

A single cymbal on a stand can be struck with a variety of different sticks or mallets, or even bowed to create a strange, creepy sound.

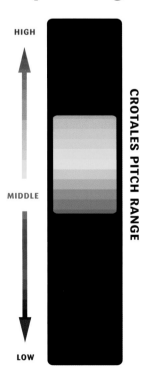

Highs & Lows pitch range

HIGH

MIDDLE

LOW

CROTALES PITCH RANGE

Did you know ?

Hi-hat cymbals are two smaller cymbals which jump up and down, clashing together, when your foot presses a pedal. They're used in jazz as part of the drumkit and occasionally seen in orchestras.

In the second millennium B.C., cymbals used to be played during wrestling matches.

 CD-ROM ▶

Hear the instruments! Click Cymbals or Crotales Sound under "Percussion"

Castanets

What are they?

Two hollow wooden or plastic shells. They're used in Spanish flamenco dancing.

In orchestral music, they can conjure up a Spanish mood.

How do you play them?

You hold the two shells in one hand and, with fast finger movement, make them clap together quickly.

What sound do they make?

An energetic "clack-clack" sound.

Did you know?

The word "castanet" comes from **"castaña"** – the Spanish for **"chestnut."**

Many civilizations believe that rattles can ward off evil spirits.

Maracas

What are they?

Maracas are rattles that come from Central America. They're often used in pairs.

They consist of round or egg-shaped containers, usually made of wood or plastic. These are filled with whatever makes the best rattle: beans, pebbles, buttons - it varies! They narrow into a thin handle for you to hold.

How do you play them?

You shake them! But there are other clever things you can do, such as:

- Twirl them to make a kind of drumroll.
- Strike one of them into your open hand.
- Flick them to create complex rhythms.

What sound do they make?

A hustling, shuffling, rattling sound.

Tam-tam

It's a fact...

Some 20th-century composers have experimented by getting the percussionist to do unusual things with a tam-tam. The American composer John Cage had it lowered into water: that makes quite an eerie sound!

What is it?

A gigantic round dish of metal, like a gong.

Tam-tams come from the Far East and Central Asia.

What sound does it make?

A loud, fantastically rich, exotic, colorful, echoing sound.

How do you play it?

You strike it with a beater that has a large, padded head.

You can even scrape it with a bouncy ball to make it sound like a dinosaur!

CD-ROM ▶

Hear the instruments! Click Castanets, Maracas, or Tam-tam Sound under "Percussion"

In Indonesia there are orchestras called **"gamelan"** orchestras. Gongs feature a lot here. All the instruments are very rich and echoey.

THE KEYBOARDS

Keyboard instruments commonly appear in concertos and chamber ensembles, as well as in jazz and pop music. They only occasionally turn up in orchestral pieces.

The harpsichord, piano and organ are completely different. They're grouped together because they all have keyboards, but each has a unique design for producing sound.

Piano

Harpsichord

Organ

The Harpsichord
Plucky Jacks-in-a-Box

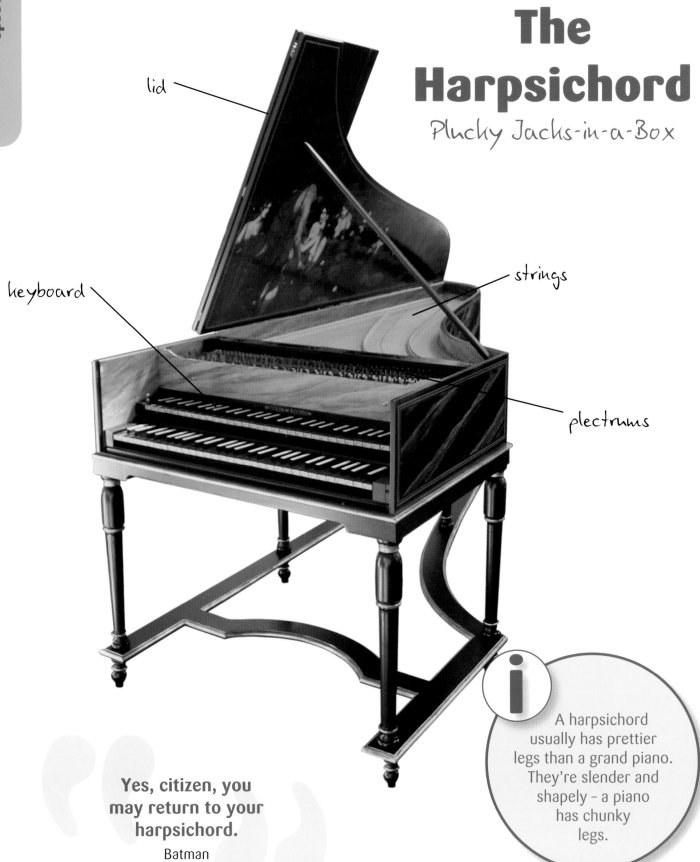

lid

keyboard

strings

plectrums

> **Yes, citizen, you may return to your harpsichord.**
> Batman

i A harpsichord usually has prettier legs than a grand piano. They're slender and shapely – a piano has chunky legs.

Overall

The twinkly, twangy sound of a harpsichord used to be everywhere in music. It's an old instrument and was once all the rage: many homes would have had one, and composers wrote for it all the time.

It spiced up the orchestra's sound and played many solo pieces.

But then the piano came along like a new kid on the block and told the harpsichord to get lost. These days, composers don't write for it very much.

Did you know ?

It's called a "**harpsichord**" because its strings are plucked, like the strings of a harp. It's like a horizontal harp in a wooden box with a keyboard!

Q **So what's it doing in this book?**

A **Well**, in the middle of the 20th century, people started to perform older music on older instruments. Instead of letting the piano play everything, they decided that the harpsichord should be given back its own music. So, if a composer in the 17th century wrote a piece including a harpsichord and it's being performed in a concert, the harpsichord comes back to play its part.

Harpsichords in the Orchestra

Music today doesn't usually need a harpsichord – but a concert of *older* music often does.

Harpsichord players are different from everyone else, for two reasons:

1) Their music often has numbers instead of notes. This is called "**figured bass**" and it tells them which chords to play. If they want to put a few extra notes in, that's fine. There's quite a lot of freedom.

2) Years ago, harpsichordists often had to **conduct** while playing the harpsichord. So today's players sometimes do the same to give the audience a flavor of how it was 200 years ago.

One or two much later composers, such as **Francis Poulenc** and Manuel de Falla, have written for the harpsichord too.

When the conductor of the orchestra also plays the harpsichord, he really has to multi-task. His fingers have to move non-stop over the keys, and whenever he can he waves an arm to remind the orchestra that he's in charge.

The harpsichord's main problem was that it couldn't vary its "dynamics" – i.e. it couldn't play more loudly or more softly. You could bash it with all the strength you'd got or touch the keys like a fairy, but it wouldn't make any difference: the volume wouldn't change. That's why the piano overtook it.

You can find harpsichords in:

Concertos: Many from the Baroque (1600-1750) and early Classical (1750-1820) eras; even one or two from the 20th century.

Chamber music: Years ago, a lot of rich families had harpsichords so plenty of chamber music was written to be played by small groups at home.

Solo pieces: No shortage of solo music by Baroque composers such as J.S. Bach, Handel and Domenico Scarlatti - Scarlatti wrote over 550 sonatas for the harpsichord!

Did you know?

On a piano, the big bottom row of keys is white and the little top row is black. On a harpsichord they're often reversed, so the big ones are black and the little ones are white.

Construction of the Harpsichord

Harpsichords have been made in all shapes and sizes. They usually have a wing-shaped **body** made of wood - like the grand piano, only not as thick and heavy. The top is a lid on hinges: it can be lifted up so that you can hear the sound more easily.

Inside the body - underneath the lid - are metal **strings**. These are plucked by a "plectrum" when you press the keys.

The **plectrum** often used to be a quill (the hard, white bit at the bottom of a bird's feather). Now it's more usually plastic. The "**jack**," that holds the plectrum, is made of wood.

There are often two "**manuals**," which means two "keyboards."

Harpsichord players don't move around much when they play. Because the harpsichord doesn't vary in volume, there's no point in swaying around on the stool and making your whole body work like a pianist does. The technique is more delicate.

Harpsichord keys

How do you play it?

The keys of a harpsichord are a bit like a see-saw. When you press down one end (the end you see on the keyboard), the other end (which you can't see) comes up. On this other end is a little piece of wood called a jack, and inside the jack is a plectrum. As the end comes up, the plectrum plucks the string.

Usually there are two or three sets of strings. This means that when you press a key, the plectrum will pluck more than one string for that note. It makes the sound a bit stronger.

Harpsichord players do a lot of trilling and twiddling. The notes don't last very long when you play them, so it helps to keep the sound alive if you "decorate" it with little notes in between the bigger ones.

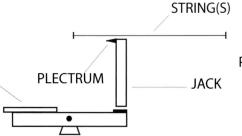

STRING(S)

KEY

PLECTRUM

JACK

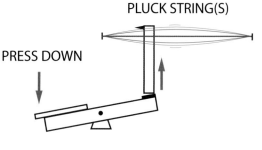

PLUCK STRING(S)

PRESS DOWN

The quill for the plectrum used to be from a large wild bird, like a raven or a crow.

Somebody once described the sound of the harpsichord as a performance on a birdcage with a toasting fork!

Highs & Lows pitch range

The range of older harpsichords will vary. But a modern harpsichord will usually manage this:

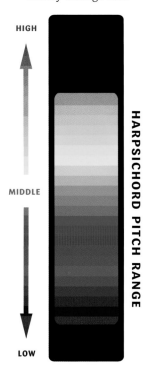

HIGH

MIDDLE

LOW

HARPSICHORD PITCH RANGE

It's a fact...

Harpsichords are often beautifully decorated. They were highly prized pieces of furniture as well as musical instruments.

Early Relations

Clavichord
Like the harpsichord, but has a weaker sound.

Virginal
An early harpsichord contained in a rectangular box with only one string per note.

Spinet
Like a virginal, but wing-shaped.

CD-ROM ▶

Hear the instruments!
Click Harpsichord
Sound under
"Keyboards"

The Pianoforte
("Piano")
The Mechanical Marvel

A grand piano can weigh more than 1,000 pounds..

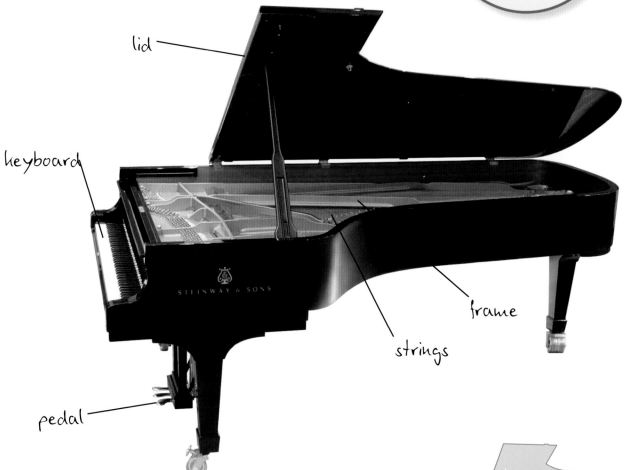

lid

keyboard

frame

strings

pedal

> **A piano is a monster that screams when you touch its teeth.**
>
> Andrés Segovia,
> classical guitarist

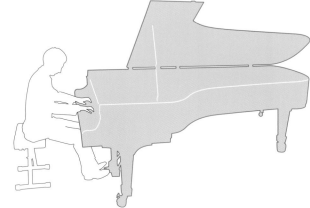

Overall

The best thing about a piano is that it can play as many notes together as you ask it to. A piano keyboard usually has 88 keys - over seven octaves. The limit is made by your body: you have only 10 fingers and thumbs, and they're not on elastic. But when you hear how the best players fly up and down the long keyboard, you'd think some of them had 20 fingers!

In many homes, the piano is part of the furniture. True, it's a bit big to be locked away in an instrument case - but you don't normally see people proudly displaying an exercise bike or a pool table in their living room. A piano is nice to look at as well as to play.

It doesn't have a naturally beautiful sound, like the violin or the cello, but the best players can make it sound beautiful.

Pianos in the Orchestra

The piano is such an amazing instrument by itself, it hardly needs an orchestra. It's not a regular member and is only occasionally found in orchestral pieces.

It's actually treated a bit like a percussion instrument: it often has bouncy, occasional bursts of notes that add to the overall sound.

Pianists are both lucky and unlucky:

 Lucky because they don't have to tune their own instrument. Other players have to tune theirs at the beginning of every concert (and sometimes in the middle too!). But a piano is so heavy and complicated it needs an expert tuner.

 Unlucky because they can't bring their own piano to a concert. Pianos are too big and heavy to be carried around. So instead of the piano they know and love, pianists have to put up with all kinds of different ones. And it's no good blaming a bad performance on the piano - because the audience won't!

Did you know ?

Alexander Graham Bell, the inventor of the telephone, was a gifted pianist. When he was a teenager he discovered that if he played a chord on a piano in one room, it would echo on a piano in another room. He realized that whole chords could be sent through the air, vibrating at exactly the same pitch. This was the beginning of his path to inventing the telephone...

Did you know ?

"Pianoforte" means "soft-loud": the piano was the first keyboard instrument that could be played very quietly or very loudly (and everything in between).

Older pianos had the name "fortepiano" rather than "pianoforte."

You'll find pianos in:

Concertos: Stacks of these, from Mozart onwards - the grand piano stands in front of the orchestra and all eyes are on the pianist.

Chamber music: There are many pieces for small groups with piano. It's also used to accompany one other instrument - such as the violin, the clarinet or the flute - in sonatas and other pieces.

Solo pieces: Plenty for pianists. Just about anyone who's anyone has written music for the piano! Chopin was an expert and *always* wrote for the piano.

Jazz: The piano doesn't just know how to be strait-laced and classical. It's very happy in the whimsical world of jazz, too, ready for fast, twiddly pieces or slow, moody ones.

Pop music: Pianos have been part of pop and rock music since their invention. From Jerry Lee Lewis or Billy Joel decades ago, to Tori Amos or Coldplay today, the piano makes regular appearances on the pop charts.

Construction of the Piano

The piano is basically a string instrument with a keyboard.

The keys used to be made of ivory, but now they're made of special plastic. The bottom row is always white, and the top row is always black.

The strings are made of steel, and the little wooden hammers that hit them are covered with felt.

A wooden "jack" connects the key to the hammer.

Underneath the strings there is a "soundboard." This is a large, thin sheet of wood that amplifies the sound of the strings. You'd hardly hear them without this. It's sometimes called the "soul" or "voice" of the piano.

Piano keys

Hammers

Soundboard (beneath strings)

The wood used for the piano's soundboard is often spruce - the same as for the front of a violin. Spruce is good at making the sound richer and warmer.

In a harpsichord, the strings are plucked by quills. But in a piano, the sound is stronger and more varied because the strings are hit by little hammers. An Italian named Cristofori invented this mechanism at the end of the 17th century - and it was a breakthrough.

There are **two** main types
of pianos today:

1) Grand pianos

Grand pianos can be "baby"
grands or "concert" grands, or
several sizes in between. For
these, the body is wing-shaped
and the strings run horizontally.

*Full-sized
concert grand
pianos are about
nine feet long.*

2) Upright pianos

Upright pianos are smaller,
and often seen in people's homes.

They're more compact because the
strings run vertically. It's like saving space
by building apartments that go up high,
instead of lots of houses that take up more land.

**Piano strings in a
"baby" grand piano
(right) and an
upright piano
(bottom right)**

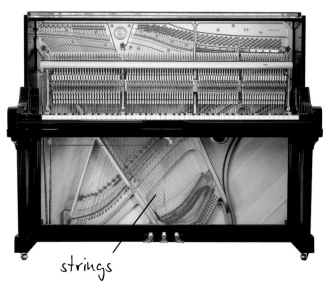

strings

There are at least two metal **pedals** on a piano, sometimes three:

i To be a good pianist, you need strong, muscular fingers.

1) Soft pedal (on the left)

On a grand piano, this moves the hammers sideways so that only one string per note (rather than the normal two or three) is hit by each hammer.

On an upright piano, the soft pedal makes the hammers move closer to the strings, so they don't take such a big swing and hit them so hard.

Either way, it gives a softer, more muffled sound.

2) Sostenuto pedal (in the middle)

This allows you to keep some notes sounding while you continue to pedal others in the normal way.

3) Sustaining pedal (on the right)

This takes the "dampers" away from the strings. It means that the strings continue to vibrate and the sound goes on for a long time.

Digital piano

The body of a piano is made from thick wood. Concert grands are normally black, but uprights can be all shades of wood. Electric pianos, used in pop music, are sometimes white.

Did you know?

There was once a "**giraffe piano**" that reached up towards the ceiling. Not surprisingly, it didn't catch on!

There are also digital pianos, which use electricity to work. They're smaller and cheaper, so they sometimes suit beginners. And you can use headphones with them, so people with neighbors find them useful for practicing! But a digital piano isn't a rival for the rich sound of a "real" piano.

How do you play it?

You sit on a stool in front of the keyboard and press the keys.

Here's what happens:

1) When you press the front of a key on the keyboard, the back of it (which you can't see when you're playing) goes up.

2) The back of the key is connected to a wooden "jack," and the jack flicks upwards.

3) This makes the hammer move towards the string.

4) The "damper," covered in felt, moves away from the string.

5) The hammer hits the string.

6) When you take your finger off the key, the damper goes back to rest on the string and stop it vibrating.

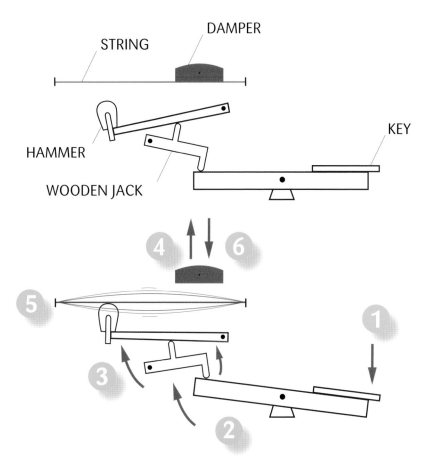

STRING   DAMPER

HAMMER

WOODEN JACK

KEY

Did you know?

A rebellious American composer called **John Cage** used to attach all kinds of bits to the strings of the piano, like rubber bands and nails, to make it sound like a weird percussion instrument. It's called "**prepared piano**" and he wrote lots of pieces for it.

CD-ROM ▶

Highs & Lows pitch range

This is for most pianos:

HIGH

MIDDLE

LOW

PIANO PITCH RANGE

People often think that to play the piano more loudly you "hit" the keys harder. It's not true! It's actually the *speed* at which the keys go down that affects the volume. If a key is pressed quickly, it's the *hammer* that will hit the *string* with more force and make a louder note come out. If *you* just hit the *keys*, you'll sound more like a gorilla playing the piano than a skilled human being...

CD-ROM ▶

Hear the instruments! Click Piano Sound under "Keyboards"

The Organ
The King of Instruments

pipes

stops

console (with different "mannals"- keyboards)

pedals

The organ was called the **"king of instruments"** as early as the 14th century.

All one has to do is hit the right notes at the right time and the instrument plays itself.

J.S. Bach,
Baroque composer

It's a fact...

The organ is such an awesome instrument, it's easy to forget the person playing it. Although you have to be very skilled to play the organ, people often can't see you. In a church or cathedral, *you* tend to be hidden away and the *pipes* get all the attention!

Sometimes it's difficult for an organist to see much except the organ, so there might be a little mirror to reflect what's going on. In a concert, it means the conductor is visible, so the organist doesn't play too slowly or too fast.

Overall

The organ is a grand keyboard instrument, with stops and pipes and pedals. There's a lot to master!

Pipes

Pedals

Manuals (keyboards)

Stops

- The **pipes** stretch up to the ceiling like an enormous radiator.

- The **pedals** are like a king-size keyboard for the feet, splaying out towards you on the floor.

- Big organs can have as many as **five keyboards** (called "manuals").

- Lots of "**stops**" are in groups to the left and right. They control which pipes make a sound. The organist pulls them out or pushes them back in to create different sound-worlds – from low, thunderous notes to high, heavenly pipes and flutes.

- The organ stops are labelled with the names of orchestral instruments, like "oboe" and "flute." When you pull out a "flute" one, the organ sounds gentle and airy, like a flute.

The organ's home is in churches, where it has lived for centuries. But sometimes it is used for different kinds of music...

Concertos: Some, especially from the Baroque era (1600–1750). Many Baroque composers were organists themselves.

Chamber music: Smaller organs (chamber organs) also form part of small groups in Baroque music.

Choral music: Used for religious choral pieces, like Bach's B minor Mass. And it's used in church services to accompany the congregation singing hymns.

Orchestra: In the orchestra the organ is a very occasional, spectacular visitor.

Solo pieces: Plenty of these for organists to enjoy.

Did you know

In a church the place where the organist sits at the keyboard is often high up and called an "**organ loft**."

Construction of the Organ

The case is wooden, the pedals are wooden, and the pipes are metal and wooden.

Highs & Lows pitch range

The pedal part for the organ is written separately. The range of the pedals alone is:

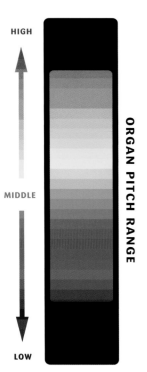

HIGH

MIDDLE

LOW

ORGAN PITCH RANGE

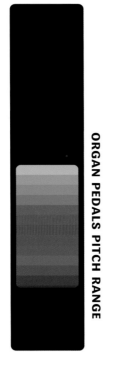

ORGAN PEDALS PITCH RANGE

How do you play it?

1) You sit at the "console," which contains all the manuals (keyboards).

2) You press the keys with your fingers and/or the pedals with your feet.

3) Air is sent through the pipes, splitting at the edge of them in a similar way to a flautist's breath on the mouthpiece of a flute.

In pre-electric times, men would be working hard behind the scenes to keep the bellows going and make this happen. Now it's all done electrically.

You have to have good co-ordination to play the organ: hands, feet and eyes all have challenging jobs to do at the same time. If you can pat your head, rub your stomach *and* stamp your feet, you might have a chance...

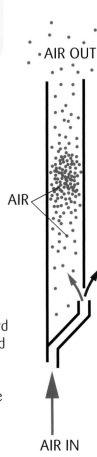

AIR OUT

AIR

AIR IN

Other Organs

Chamber organ

Sometimes, people need an organ that isn't installed like a monster in a church. When they do, they might use a chamber organ. This has just one manual and no pedals.

Harmonium

This is a little organ that uses metal reeds instead of pipes to produce the sound. Air is created by bellows that are operated by hand or by a foot-pump.

The harmonium is no longer used very much, except in India. They were taken there by missionaries in the 19th century.

Accordion

This is the smallest and oldest member of the organ family. You create the air by pulling out and pushing in the two sides: the bellows are folded – in pleats, like a fan – in the middle. You press buttons, or keys on a keyboard, for different notes.

The accordion is found in a lot of folk music.

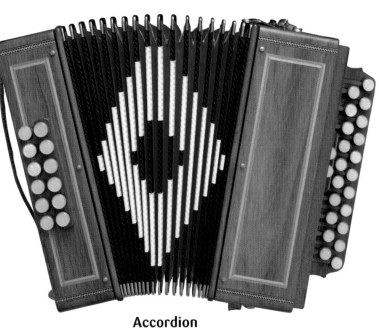

Accordion

The harmonica is the world's best-selling instrument.

Harmonica
or "mouth organ"

The harmonica isn't much bigger than a candy bar and doesn't have a keyboard, so it's not an organ in the normal sense.

To play it, you cover the little holes with your mouth and breathe alternately out – *and in*! It takes time to master that. Little metal reeds vibrate inside its small, narrow box. By sliding the harmonica left or right and moving your head slightly, your mouth covers different holes so different notes sound.

Some famous composers have written for the harmonica – Vaughan Williams wrote *Romance for Harmonica, Strings and Piano in D flat major*.

♪ CD-ROM ▶

Hear the instruments! Click Organ Sound under "Keyboards"

The Voice

The Most Natural Instrument in the World

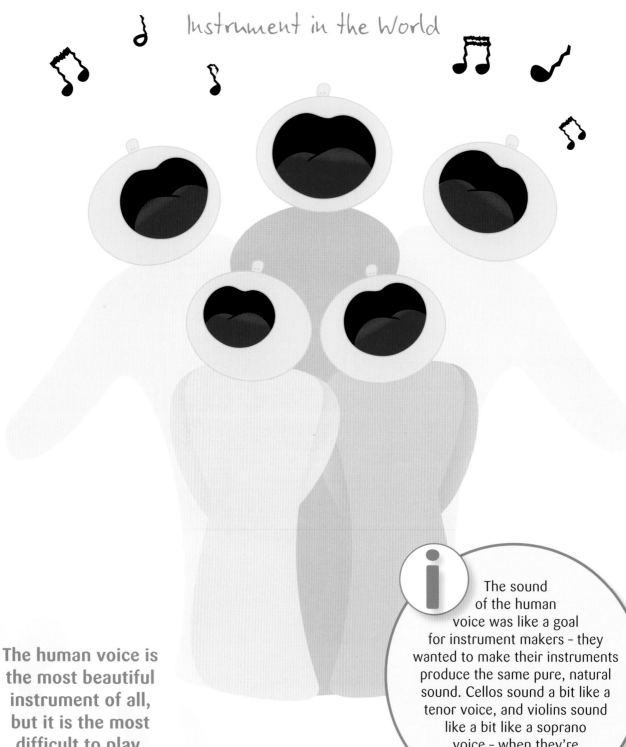

The human voice is the most beautiful instrument of all, but it is the most difficult to play.

Richard Strauss, composer

The sound of the human voice was like a goal for instrument makers – they wanted to make their instruments produce the same pure, natural sound. Cellos sound a bit like a tenor voice, and violins sound like a bit like a soprano voice – when they're played well!

Overall

The voice is the oldest instrument of all. It's used everywhere in the world. It doesn't cost money. You don't need a case to put it in. You don't have to polish it, make reeds for it, get strings for it, or put it together. Great!

But actually, the voice isn't so different from later inventions. It has a body and strings (vocal chords): so does a violin. You take a big breath to produce a long note: so does a wind player. But you don't need keys, valves, a bow or a beater to make your voice work.

The voice has lots of music to sing:

- **Opera:** like musical theater, with showy solos.
- **Songs:** classical, jazz, pop, folk etc., for one or two voices.
- **Choral music:** for choirs, with occasional solos. Choral works often have religious words.

Sometimes the voice sings with the orchestra. There are many songs, and occasionally sections of symphonies, which have just one voice singing with all the other instruments. When the composer writes good music and the singer is well-trained, the voice can easily be heard.

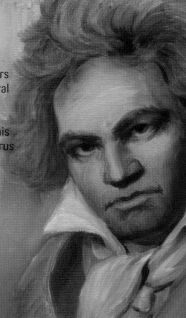

Choirs

A choir, or chorus, is a group of voices. Choirs often go together with orchestras: most choral music needs an orchestra with it, and some composers have even written choral parts for their symphonies. Beethoven did it with his magnificent Ninth Symphony, where the chorus sings "Ode to Joy" in the last movement.

A lot of choirs aren't professional. Many people can sing quite well, and singing together with others can be really satisfying. So there are countless amateur choirs.

Training

To be a really good singer you need proper training. We all have a voice, but it doesn't mean we know how to use it well. If you were born with a violin under your chin, you'd still need to learn how to play it!

Part of the training is to stop you straining your vocal chords. If you sing a lot, and you don't know how to do it properly, you can damage your voice. It's important to support the breath with your diaphragm muscle, just like a wind player does.

There are different types of choirs:

- Church choirs
- Symphony choruses (very big!)
- Chamber choirs (fewer people)
- Male choirs (men only)
- Female choirs (women only)
- Barbershop quartets (these sing without accompaniment)
- Operatic choruses (various sizes, depending on the opera)

"**Vocalise**" is a kind of singing with no words. The voice is treated just like an instrument of the orchestra. Some composers even ask singers to imitate instruments - the opposite of instruments being made to sound like the voice!

Voice Types

Here are the different types of voice in order from the highest in pitch to the lowest:

Soprano
- Woman or girl (boy is called "treble")
- The highest voice

Treble – boy soprano
- Boy
- Same as the female soprano, but with a purer, clearer sound. Often found in church choirs

Mezzo-soprano
- Woman
- Between the soprano and alto in pitch

Contralto ("Alto")
- Usually a woman (a man is called a "countertenor")
- Second-highest in a four-part choir

Did you know ?

A choir is usually in **four** parts: **soprano** (highest), **alto** (a bit lower), **tenor** (lower still), **bass** (lowest). Sometimes each of these will split again into two more parts for singing complicated music with lots of lines. And sometimes there are voices pitched in between the main ones, called mezzo-soprano and baritone.

Here, you can compare all the vocal pitch ranges and see how the choir is built, from top to bottom.

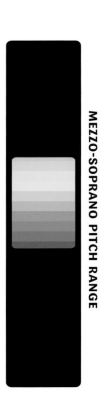

HIGH

MIDDLE

LOW

SOPRANO PITCH RANGE

MEZZO-SOPRANO PITCH RANGE

Countertenor

- Man
- Same as female alto but often with a purer, more penetrating sound

Tenor

- Man
- Second-lowest in a four-part choir

Baritone

- Man
- Between the tenor and bass in pitch

Bass

- Man
- Lowest voice of all

CD-ROM ▶

Hear the instruments! Click Sound under "Voice"

Opera singers can use a lot of **vibrato** when they sing. That's when they wobble backwards and forwards on the note, to make it sound richer. Bad ones sometimes wobble so much, you wonder which note they're actually trying to sing!

Singers have to sing in many different languages. Pronunciation is very important. A voice might be easier to carry around than a tuba, but at least a tuba player doesn't have to play in Russian!

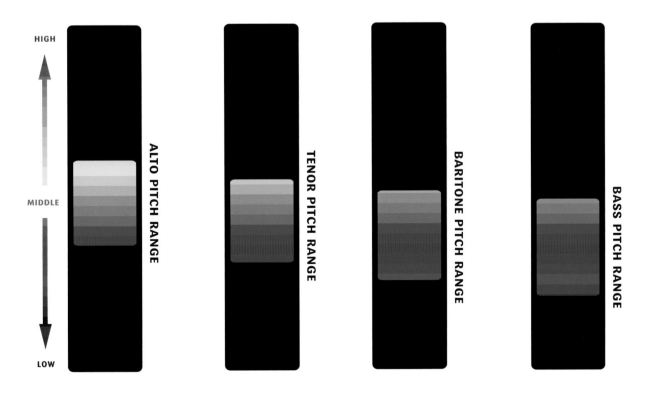

HIGH

MIDDLE

LOW

ALTO PITCH RANGE

TENOR PITCH RANGE

BARITONE PITCH RANGE

BASS PITCH RANGE

Electronic Instruments

The Weird Ones

Strange things started happening in the 20th century.
And this was *before* we met Harry Potter...

The development of electronics found its way into music. Inventors saw that there were new ways to make new sounds – *completely* new sounds. Here's just a taste of what was invented in the 20th century.

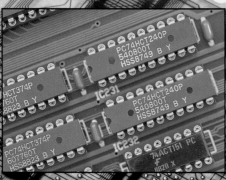

> I conceived of an instrument that would create sound without using any mechanical energy, like the conductor of an orchestra.
>
> Leon Theremin,
> inventor of the theremin

Theremin

First demonstrated: 1920
Invented by: Leon Theremin

This was one of the earliest electronic instruments, and many later ones were based on it.

It makes weird, spooky, unnatural sounds - the sort that you might hear in an early science-fiction film.

The French composer **Edgard Varèse** included the theremin in his *Ecuatorial*.

Did you know?

You can play it without touching it at all! It has two metal antennas poking out of the top, one for pitch and one for volume. You wave your hands in front of the antennae and out come strange sounds. That's because your hands are in a "magnetic field." It's called "space control." Pretty wacky...

Leon Theremin himself playing his invention

Ondes Martenot

Invented: **1928**
By: **Maurice Martenot**

The ondes martenot is like a theremin, but better! It produces similar creepy, wavering sounds, but has a keyboard and a slide.

"Ondes" means "**waves**" in French – the instrument produces wavering sounds.

It was invented in France, and the famous French composer Olivier Messiaen used the ondes martenot in many pieces, including his *Turangalîla-symphonie* (1946–8).

CD-ROM ▶

Hear the instruments! Click Ondes Martenot Sound under "Electronic Instruments"

Ondes martenot played by Sistine Martenot, Maurice's sister

Did you know?
The ondes martenot was used in the famous science-fiction series on television, **Star Trek**.

The ondes martenot has also been used for the soundtracks of many films, particularly horror and science fiction. It's still popular today: the 2001 film *Amélie* uses it, so it's not ready for the scrap heap yet.

Synthesizer

Here's a name to remember: **Dr Moog**. He's not a cartoon character, but was actually a clever inventor of electronic instruments.

Moog synthesizer

Musique concrète

In the late 1940s, something called *musique concrète* was developed by Pierre Schaeffer. Tape recording had just been invented, and Mr Schaeffer decided that he could have fun with it. This is what he did:

1) He taped all sorts of everyday sounds, like voices, cars, laughter or even footsteps.

2) He changed these sounds electronically so that they sounded strange and it was harder to tell what they were.

3) He molded his new sounds together in a sort of "musical" mosaic.

Beethoven and Mozart this certainly was *not*! But it played an important part in the process of musical composition breaking free from old rules and patterns. Why did composers have to write nice, pretty little tunes? Answer: they didn't!

A synthesizer is an electronic instrument with a keyboard. The first successful one was the Moog Synthesizer, made by Dr Robert Moog. His invention appealed to lots of people because it had a piano-style keyboard, which was familiar to them.

By the 1970s, many people, including rock musicians, were buying synthesizers: *anyone* could make weird sounds!

It's a fact...

In 1970 Dr Moog made a **"Minimoog"**! You guessed it: it's a small version of the Moog synthesizer. Many people bought one.

Digital synthesizer

Digital Synthesis

In the 1970s there was another step forward: digital synthesis. Electronic instruments up until this point had a limited range of sounds. Digital synthesis meant that it was possible to go out, record real sounds, and reproduce them on just one instrument. Instrument makers can record the mixed sound of a whole choir, for example, and transfer it into their instrument. They might then make a button labelled "choir": once you've pressed the button, each note that you play sounds like a choir is singing it!

Computer Music

The computer is an instrument too!

Computers have become a key part of our world. They're used for fun and for work, and they can play back music that has been recorded.

These days, they're also an important tool for composers. Just as you can type words on a screen, you can also type musical notes. So composers don't always use manuscript paper and a pencil anymore.

Composers can even create new sounds using computer equipment. They can alter them, combine them, and even use them alongside traditional orchestral sounds.

In 1983 **MIDI** was introduced (MIDI = Musical Instrument Digital Interface). It became a standard way of linking up digital instruments with each other and with computers. Technology was getting more and more advanced – and still is.

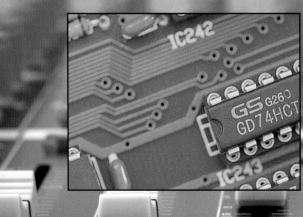

**Connecting tracks
of a circuit board**

Will computers take over?

If computers are so clever, will there be no need for instruments?
Here are some reasons why the instruments' future looks good:

- Synthesizers and computers can *imitate* instruments, but they're still no substitute for the real thing. The sounds are not nearly as rich, distinctive or subtle.

- What about books? You can read text on a screen but in the end it's nice to handle a book and see the words on paper. It's like that with musical instruments. And if you go to a concert, it's not only the *sound* of an orchestra that is unique: it's what it looks like!

- Computers are a bit too precise. Musical performance is special because it's never the same twice. Human beings interact with each other and produce something slightly different each time they perform the same piece. That's why it's entertaining. We'd need a collection of really amazing robots before we could imitate that...

- Computers can be perfect: no wrong notes, no need to practice. But in the end, we find perfection boring. A performance isn't so exciting without the chance that someone might mess it up!

So although technology will get better and better, true musical instruments will continue to thrive, as will the orchestra – the most spectacular instrument of them all.

Did you know ?

In his opera *The Mask of Orpheus*, completed in 1975, **Harrison Birtwistle** uses computer-generated harp sounds. This was a new development for the traditional world of opera!

The Conductor
Boss with the Baton

Marin Alsop

Simon Rattle

Not all conductors use a baton - some just use their hands.

Overall

So just *what* is all this arm-waving about?
Is it *really* necessary?
And how difficult is it?

A conductor is an instrument, too! Nearly all orchestras today have conductors. They're the ones who stand on their own at the front of the orchestra. They have their back to you, and seem to be doing something that looks like traffic control with a stick.

Orchestras could play without conductors, but they wouldn't be as good. The conductor leads the players, encourages them, keeps them together, and makes sure every single musician has the same idea about the music and performs it in the same way.

Some conductors conduct the music from memory, with no score on their stand. They memorize every single orchestral part - that's a lot to carry in your brain! It's something like memorizing the lines from an entire play - not just for one role, but for them all. Could you do that?

What else does the conductor do?

- Helps to choose which pieces the orchestra should play.

- Attends all the rehearsals. Some conductors make musicians work really hard, and single them out if they play incorrectly. Some talk a lot. Some shout a lot. Just like school teachers!

- Takes responsibility for how good the performance is. It's like school exams: if a class does well, it makes the teacher look good; if a class does badly, people wonder if it's the teacher's fault. The same goes for an orchestra and its conductor.

You can beat with your fingers, wrist, your eyes, foot, it really doesn't matter, as long as you have imagination and know what you want.

Georg Solti,
famous conductor

Jean-Baptiste Lully

Before conductors as we know them today, somebody often beat time by banging a big stick on the floor. Imagine how annoying it was to listen to a piece of music with "THUMP... THUMP... THUMP" all the way through it. **Jean-Baptiste Lully**, a French composer of the Baroque era, proved what a bad idea it was: he banged the stick right down on his foot and died from his wound!

How does a conductor conduct?

It isn't just the hands that a conductor uses:
it's the whole body.

FACE
The expression on a conductor's face is very important. **Eyes** are especially useful: they not only read the music and look around, but they can silently communicate a lot to the musicians.

MOUTH
Conductors talk a lot in rehearsals, and sometimes they shout. In *concerts*, of course, the conductor's mouth has less to do. If the orchestra still needs to be told things at that stage, the performance is in trouble!

RIGHT HAND
This hand controls the beat.

ARMS
The way the conductor's arms move is as important as the hands on the end of them!

LEFT HAND
This hand tells players when to come in, and how much volume and expression to play with.

LEGS & FEET
Some conductors bounce around more than others, but most move a bit as they tell the musicians what to do.

It's a fact...

Notice that the conductor is the only individual *person* whom we talk about in the orchestra. We don't talk about the conductor's *baton*, like the oboist's *oboe*: we talk about the *conductor*. That's because the conductor is the boss, so his or her personality is much more important than that of an oboist, or a cellist, or any other player.

> Some conductors are composers too, as Leonard Bernstein was. Many also play instruments, often starting as pianists. And our own Marin Alsop plays the violin.

Do conductors really make a difference to the sound?

Yes! One conductor can make a whole piece sound serious and slow, and another can make the same piece sound faster and more cheerful. They must *know* how they want a piece to sound, and get the orchestra to play it that way.

One conductor might say: "Cellos: stronger here, please, and violins softer!" so that we hear the bass line more. But another conductor might say: "Cellos: softer here, please. Violins: more presence, really make the melody *sing*. And brass... be *quiet*!"

The Beat

Part of the conductor's job is to "beat time." When a piece is "in $\frac{3}{4}$", for example, there are three beats in a bar – and the conductor will beat "in three." All the players watch and keep together.

Sometimes, especially in more complicated, modern music, the conductor has to change the beat from $\frac{4}{4}$ to $\frac{5}{8}$ to $\frac{7}{4}$ etc., or beat one rhythm with the right hand and a different one with the left. It needs physical co-ordination as well as a good brain!

Did you know ?

Different conductors have different styles of conducting. Some are quite jerky and lively; some have smooth, flowing movements.

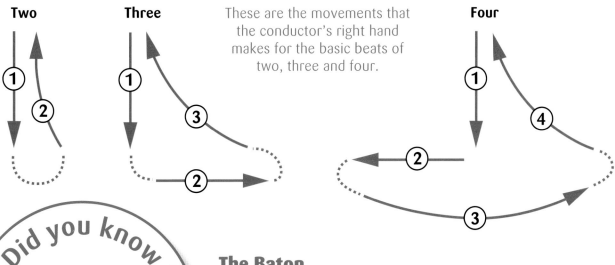

Two   **Three**

These are the movements that the conductor's right hand makes for the basic beats of two, three and four.

Four

Did you know ?

In France, a baton is called a "**baguette**." But it doesn't mean that French conductors stand there waving a bread-stick in the air!

The Baton

The baton is the little stick that most conductors wave around when they conduct.

Not all batons are the same. Some conductors like short ones, with just a little stick coming out of the end that they hold. Others prefer quite long sticks.

Some conductors don't use batons at all: they just wave their hands around and make faces.

Do conductors ever drop the baton?

Occasionally, in the excitement of a performance, the conductor loses his or her grip on the baton and it goes flying. But as far as we know, no orchestral musician has been stabbed by one.

So what happens?

The music carries on! How come? Because:

1) The conductor can still beat time using just hands.
2) Most good orchestras can manage without a conductor for a bit if they have to. The trick is to follow the first violin: the concert master, also known as the leader of the orchestra.

Richard Strauss, a great conductor as well as a famous composer, had this advice:

"Remember that you are making music not to amuse yourself, but to delight your audience."

DICTIONARY
A handy list of words and their meanings

a. = adjective
n. = noun
v. = verb
abb. = abbreviation

All underlined words have their own entry in the dictionary.

A

accompaniment music that supports the main melody

acoustic non-electric

alto the second-highest voice in a four-part choir

amplify make louder

aria solo song (also called "air"), generally as part of an opera, oratorio or cantata

authentic see "period performance"

B

bar see measure

baritone male voice between tenor and bass in pitch

Baroque era the era of western classical music, from roughly 1600 to 1750

bass 1) the bottom of the music in terms of pitch; 2) the lowest voice in a four-part choir; 3) abbreviation of "double bass"

bass line the lowest line of music in a piece

beat 1) the basic pulse of the music; 2) the movement of a hand or baton by the conductor to indicate the pulse

brass the group of instruments in the orchestra or wind band made of brass, i.e. trumpet, trombone, horn, tuba

C

cadenza a relatively brief, often showy solo in a concerto or operatic aria

cantata a work usually for solo singers, chorus and orchestra (from the Latin "cantare," to sing)

chamber music   music for small groups of players, such as a <u>string quartet</u> or a piano <u>trio</u>; so called because it was originally played in the "chamber" or home

choir   a group of singers, often divided into <u>soprano</u>, <u>alto</u>, <u>tenor</u>, <u>bass</u>

chord   two or more notes played or sung together

chorus   1) as <u>choir</u>; 2) a refrain: a recurring line or <u>phrase</u> in a choral <u>piece</u> with verses in between

chromatic   including <u>semitones</u> as well as <u>tones</u>

col legno   when <u>string</u> players use the back of the bow – the wood – to play on the strings

Classical era   the era of western <u>classical music</u>, roughly from 1750 to 1820

classical music   generally, in the western tradition, <u>acoustic</u> music which may still be performed years after it was written; therefore music in which the <u>composer</u> is as important, often more important, than the performer

clef   the sign at the beginning of a <u>staff</u> (or <u>stave</u>) that denotes the <u>pitch</u> of its lines and spaces

coda   the last part of a <u>piece</u>

composer   somebody who writes music

composition   the process of writing music; a <u>piece</u> of music

concerto   a <u>work</u> for solo <u>instrument</u> and <u>orchestra</u>, generally in three <u>movements</u> (fast-slow-fast)

conductor   the person who directs an <u>orchestra</u>

D

diaphragm   muscular sheet at the bottom of the lungs which is contracted to help the lungs expand – used a lot by <u>wind</u> players and singers

double-stopping   sounding two strings at once on an <u>instrument</u> in the <u>violin family</u>

double-tonguing   a technique used by <u>wind</u> players for playing fast music

duet, duo   1) a <u>work</u> for two players or singers; 2) a group of two players or singers

dynamics   the levels of quietness and loudness, and the terms (usually in Italian) that indicate them (*pianissimo*, *fortissimo* etc.)

F

family   a group of <u>instruments</u> of similar material, appearance and/or method of sound production

finale   the term for "last <u>movement</u>"

flat 1) a sign to the left of a note, showing it must be lowered by a <u>semitone</u>; 2) a term meaning the <u>intonation</u> is below the notated <u>pitch</u>

flutter-tonguing a fluttering sound made by <u>wind</u> players, particularly flautists

folk music the traditional music of a particular area or country, passed down through generations, often orally

G

glissando a swooping up or down of sound

H

harmony the combining of notes to make <u>chords</u>: these "vertical" chords often accompany a "horizontal" <u>melody</u> – as in a hymn

harmonic 1) *a.* describing <u>harmony</u>; 2) *n.* often plural: the airy notes that <u>violin family</u> <u>instruments</u> can produce when players touch the strings lightly in certain places

I

improvise (*n.* improvisation) to make up music as you go along, often taking a well-known tune as a starting point

instrument in music, something that produces musical sounds by <u>vibration</u>, such as a violin, clarinet, trumpet etc.

interval the distance in <u>pitch</u> between notes. For example, the interval between C and G is a fifth (C(1), D(2), E(3), F(4), G(5))

intonation the "tuning" – whether the notes are exactly in <u>tune</u>, or are <u>sharp</u> or <u>flat</u>

J

jazz a music created mainly by black Americans in the early 20th century, mixing together elements of European-American and tribal African musics; developed into many different forms, generally more relaxed than <u>classical music</u>

K

key <u>pieces</u> of western <u>classical music</u> are usually in particular keys, based on the notes of the western <u>scale</u> (C <u>major</u>, G <u>minor</u> etc.); a key is a piece's home – the music can travel away from it, but usually comes back in the end (also see "<u>tonality</u>")

keyboard instruments <u>instruments</u> with a keyboard, such as the harpsichord, piano, organ

M

major refers to the key of a piece of music – major usually sounds happier than minor

manual keyboard for the hands to play (esp. in reference to the organ)

manuscript the composer's original handwritten music

mass the worship ceremony of the Christian church; many composers have written masses

measure (UK: bar) written music is divided into "bars" or "measures" marked by vertical lines

Medieval music music before c. 1490

melody (*adj.* melodic) tune – normally the top line in a piece

mezzo-soprano female voice between soprano and alto in pitch

meter, time (*adj.* metrical) the grouping together of beats in recurrent units of two, three, four, six etc.

minor refers to the key of a piece of music – minor usually sounds sadder than major

movement a large, complete section in a symphony, chamber, choral or solo work (normally there are three or four)

mute *n.* a device used to soften the sound of an instrument (but not stop it completely); *v.* to soften the sound of an instrument

N

notation a system for writing down music

O

octave 1) the simultaneous sounding of any note with its nearest namesake, up or down (C to C, F to F etc.)

2) any range of eight notes in sequence, such as C-D-E-F-G-A-B-C

octet a work for eight players; a group of eight players

opera a stage work that combines words, drama, music (with singers and orchestra) and scenery

opus (*abb.* op.) "work" in Latin: composers' works are organized in "opus" numbers; usually the lower the opus number, the earlier in the composer's life the work was written

oratorio an extended musical setting of a religious text for performance on a concert stage by singers and orchestra; Handel's *Messiah* is a famous example

orchestra an organized body of bowed string instruments, usually with woodwind, brass and percussion

N O P Q R S T U V W X Y Z

orchestration the selection of different <u>instruments</u> in the <u>orchestra</u> to play different parts of a <u>piece</u> (a flute for this line, perhaps the cellos for that one, etc.) – thus creating a particular overall sound-world; some <u>pieces</u> originally for piano have then been "orchestrated" – different notes are given to different orchestral instruments, so it is the same piece but has a richer, fuller sound

overture a short orchestral <u>piece</u> at the beginning of an <u>opera</u>, often containing a foretaste of the opera's main <u>melodies</u>; also an independent orchestral piece, but generally descriptive of a place or an event

P

period performance the performance of music in the style of the <u>composer's</u> time: for example, instead of playing Bach's keyboard music on a piano it is played more "authentically" on a harpsichord, as it would have been at the time he wrote it

percussion a group of <u>instruments</u>, both tuned (different <u>pitches</u> available) and untuned (fixed pitch), that provide strong <u>rhythmic</u> support and interesting sound "color" for a <u>work</u>; generally, these instruments are struck to make them sound

phrase a musical sentence, or part of a sentence: a smallish group of notes or <u>measures</u> that can be played or sung in one breath: e.g. "Twinkle, twinkle, little star" (phrase one) "How I wonder what you are" (phrase two)

phrasing shaping a <u>piece</u> of music into <u>phrases</u>

piece a musical <u>composition</u>, e.g. a song, an <u>overture</u>, a <u>trio</u>, a <u>sonata</u> etc.

pitch whether notes are low or high

pizzicato plucked (<u>strings</u>)

portamento an audible "bend" in <u>pitch</u>, up or down – gliding from one note to the next without a break in the sound

prelude literally, a <u>piece</u> that is heard first and introduces another piece (like an <u>overture</u>); however, the name has been applied (most famously by Bach and Chopin) to describe freestanding short pieces

pulse same as <u>beat</u> – a usually regular, <u>rhythmic</u> anchor within a <u>piece</u> of music

Q

quartet a <u>work</u> for four players; a group of four players

quintet a <u>work</u> for five players; a group of five players

ABCDEFGHIJKL

R

range the <u>pitch</u> compass that an <u>instrument</u> can cover, from its lowest to its highest notes

register 1) as in "<u>range</u>"; 2) a particular section of an <u>instrument's</u> range

Renaissance era the era of western <u>classical music</u>, roughly from 1490 to 1600

Requiem a <u>mass</u> for the dead

resonance (*v.* **resonate)** the continuance and/or amplification of sound through <u>vibration</u> in a hollow space

rest *n.* a sign in music <u>notation</u> that indicates the absence of a sounding note; *v.* when the player stops playing in response to this sign

rhythm (*v.* **rhythmic)** the grouping of musical sounds by duration (lengths of notes) and stress (leaning into certain notes); rhythmic music makes this grouping very obvious

ricochet when the bow of a <u>violin family</u> <u>instrument</u> is thrown at the string so that it rebounds quickly

Romantic era the era of western <u>classical music</u>, roughly from 1820 to 1910

S

scale from the Italian word "scala" ("ladder") – a series of next-door notes (C–D–E–F–G–A etc.), moving up or down; these "ladders" contain the basic ingredients from which <u>melodies</u> are made and <u>keys</u> established

score the music of a <u>piece</u> written out on the page with a separate line for each <u>instrument</u>

semitone half a <u>tone</u>; the smallest <u>interval</u> in western <u>classical music</u>

septet a <u>work</u> for seven players; a group of seven players

sextet a <u>work</u> for six players; a group of six players

sharp a sign to the left of a note, showing it must be raised by a <u>semitone</u>; also a term meaning the <u>intonation</u> is above the notated <u>pitch</u>

sonata a <u>piece</u> normally for piano, or one <u>orchestral</u> <u>instrument</u> and piano, in <u>sonata form</u>

sonata form a complicated structure for <u>pieces</u> used by <u>composers</u> from the <u>Classical period</u> to the late 19th century. Basically it consists of three sections: the "exposition," "development" and "recapitulation." The exposition is where we meet the main <u>themes</u>, the development is where they go exploring, and the recapitulation is where they come back home again; there is often a <u>coda</u> at the end

soprano the highest voice in a four-part <u>choir</u>

spiccato short, bouncy strokes played in the middle of the bow on <u>violin family</u> <u>instruments</u>

staccato short, bouncy notes

staff (UK: stave)	the set of five lines on which notes of music are written in <u>notation</u>
string family	violin, viola, cello and double bass (though the double bass is slightly different from the others), as well as harp and guitar
string instruments	<u>instruments</u> sounded by the vibration of strings
sul ponticello	<u>violin family</u> <u>instruments</u> playing right next to the bridge
symphony	1) originally, a word meaning sounds going well together; 2) later, a large, important <u>work</u> for orchestra in different <u>movements</u>, some fast, some slow; the first movement is often in <u>sonata form</u>
symphony orchestra	the main kind of <u>orchestra</u> in western <u>classical music</u> that developed in Europe in the 18th century
syncopation	accents falling on irregular <u>beats</u>, generally giving a "swinging" feel; often found in <u>jazz</u>

T

technique	physical skill in playing an <u>instrument</u>
tempo	the speed of a <u>piece</u> of music
tenor	the second-lowest voice in a four-part <u>choir</u>
tension	how tight or loose something is (for <u>strings</u>, tighter means a higher <u>pitch</u>; looser means a lower pitch)
theme	usually, a recognizable <u>melody</u> on which a <u>piece</u> is based
time	see "<u>meter</u>"
timbre, tone color	the property of sound that distinguishes a horn from a piano, a violin from a xylophone etc.
transposing	changing <u>key</u>
transposing instruments	<u>instruments</u> that are naturally in a different <u>key</u> from that of C; for more detail, see "Transposing Instruments" on the CD-ROM
triple-stopping	sounding three strings at once on an instrument in the <u>violin family</u>
tonality (key)	tonality is like a musical solar system in which each note (or "planet"), each rung of the <u>scale</u>, has a relationship with one particular note (or "sun"), which is known as the "key-note" or "tonic." This is the music's home: it begins here, and comes back here at the end. When this planetary system is based on the note C, the key-note, or tonic, is C and the music is said to be "in the <u>key</u> of C." The <u>composer</u> can move to

other keys (modulation) which sometimes creates a feeling of unrest: this is resolved when the music comes back to the key in which it started

tone 1) describes a player's sound; 2) a "major second" interval – the sum of two semitones

treble 1) the top of the music in terms of pitch; 2) boy soprano

tremolo a "trembling" sound made by string players when they move the bow backwards and forwards very fast on a single pitch

trill a fast alternation of two next-door notes

trio a work for three players; a group of three players

triple-stopping an instrument from the violin family sounding three strings at once

tune 1) *n.* see "melody"; 2) *v.* to adjust an instrument so that it matches the standard pitch that everyone must stick to, and is not flat or sharp

V

variation when a composer writes a tune and then composes various different versions of it, decorating it and probably changing the speed – a bit like dressing up a person in various clothes: the person is the same underneath but looks different (here, the tune is the same underneath, but sounds different)

vibration (*v.* vibrate) the cause of all sound; very rapid movement of something, like the vibration of a string, the vibration of a wind player's lips or the vibration of air down a woodwind or brass instrument

vibrato a wobbling of the note backwards and forwards very quickly to make the overall sound a bit richer (the sound "vibrates")

virtuoso a musician of exceptional technical skill

W

wind instruments instruments belonging to the woodwind and brass families

wind band a group consisting of brass and woodwind instruments only

woodwind instruments which are blown and (at least originally) were made of wood, such as the flute, oboe, clarinet and bassoon

work a musical piece, often quite long and sometimes in several movements

world music music from all over the world that is not part of the western classical tradition

NOPQRSTUVWXYZ

INDEX

Acknowledgments

All page references and credits for illustrations below.

bn = bassoon; cl = clarinet; db = double bass; eh = English horn; fl = flute; glock = glockenspiel; gui = guitar; hn = horn; hpd = harpsichord; ma = marimba; ob = oboe; om = ondes martenot; perc = percussion; pf = piano; pic = piccolo; timp = timpani; tmbe = tambourine; trbn = trombone; tpt = trumpet; va = viola; vc = cello; vib = vibraphone; vn = violin; xyl = xylophone

Karen Aplin: p. 41 (German bow hold)
Vincent Bach: pp. 10 (tuba), 11 (tuba), 12 (hn), 13 (hn), 17 (tuba, pic), 50 (fl, ob), 51 (pic), 53 (ob), 57 (fl), 60 (pic), 62 (ob), 86 (tpt, trbn), 87 (hn, tuba), 90 (hn), 91 (tpt), 93 (tpt), 96 (pic tpt, cornet), 97 (pic tpt, cornet), 98 (trbn), 102 (trbns), 104 (hn), 105 (fl, ob), 107 (tuba), 108 (tuba), 110 (tuba), 119 (tpt)
Grammenos Chalkias: p. 71 (playing cl)
Hannah Davies: pp. 16 (playing ob), 19 (vc), 20 (scroll & bow), 23 (vc), 34-7 (vc), 53 (sax reed), 61 (fl keys), 65 (playing ob), 66 (playing eh, eh bottom), 70 (cl in parts), 88 (playing tpt), 165 (baton); all pitch diagrams
Jupiter di Medici: p. 60 (alto fl), 61 (bass fl)
Dreamstime: p. 47
Ralf Ehlers: p. 23 (bows)
EMI Classics / Peter Adamik: p. 162 (Simon Rattle)
Adrian France: p. 101 (sackbut)
Genevieve Helsby: pp. 18, 23, 38 (db)
Rebecca Helsby: p. 160 (manuscript)
iStockphoto: pp. 10 (vn), 12 (vn), 13 (tmbe), 14 (vn), 16 (cymbal, violinist), 20 (bow & arrow), 42 (harp strings), 43 (harp), 44 (harp), 45 (harp strings), 46 (plectrums, flag), 47 (plucking guitar), 48 (almonds), 59 (flautist, bottle), 60 (salt & pepper), 64 (pastoral scene), 68 (cat), 75 (roots), 77 (reeds), 78 (measuring tape), 80 (dollars), 84 (recorder), 93 (Tutankhamun), 94 (crown), 100

(motorbike), 103 (measuring tape), 105 (hooves), 106 (ink), 107 (hose), 112 (hands), 121 (beaters), 126 (typewriter), 127 (sticks, brushes), 130 (tmbe played), 131 (triangle, beaters), 132 (cymbal & stick), 134 (chestnuts), 135 (ball), 140 (hpd), 143 (pf hands), 144 (keys x 2, soundboard), 145 (strings in baby grand), 146 (giraffe), 149 (pipes, stops), 151 (accordion, harmonica), 152 (voices), 160 (synthesizer, computer keys), 161 (tracks), 164 (conductor)
Arthur Ka Wai Jenkins: pp. 8 (timp), 11 (snare drum, beaters), 12 (snare drum, vib), 18 (harp), 20 (harpist), 42 (harp), 44 (pedals), 46 (gui), 50 (bn), 51 (cbn), 55 (bns), 63 (tuning fork), 66 (eh), 74 (bn), 78 (cbn), 85 (recorders), 88 (mute), 96 (timp), 112 (all perc), 116 (all perc), 117 (beaters), 118 (timp), 119 (timp pedal), 121 (xyl), 122 (ma, glock), 123 (vib, vib discs), 124 (tubular bells), 125 (celesta), 126 (all perc), 127 (snare drum), 128 (bass drum), 129 (tom-toms), 130 (bongos, tmbe still), 131 (wood block), 132 (cymbals still), 133 (crotales), 134 (castanets, maracas), 135 (tam-tam), 136 (pf), 137 (organ), 142 (pf), 148 (organ), 149 (pedals, manuals), 177 (author); diagrams pp. 17, 22, 52, 56, 71, 77, 88, 89, 141, 149, 165
A.J. Lacey: p. 32 (viola d'amore – instrument currently owned by Oliver Weber)
Colin Lawson: p. 71 (chalumeau)
Lebrecht Music & Arts Photo Library: p. 21 (Stradivari), 27 (Paganini), 40 (viol), 53 (bassoon reed), 67 (ob d'amore), 76 (crook & reed), 107 (Wagner tuba), 113 (EG x 2), 119 (beaters), 156 (om), 157 (theremin), 158 (om), 159 (moog)
Grant Leighton: p. 4-6, 162 (Marin Alsop)
Tony Morrell: all drawings of instrumental players
Naxos.com (Ken Fung Choi): pp. 32 (Mozart), 33 (Berlioz), 57 (Debussy), 63 (Prokofiev), 67 (Ravel), 94 (Mozart), 97 (Verdi), 120 (Berlioz), 121 (Saint-Saëns), 139 (Falla), 147 (Cage), 153 (Beethoven), 163 (Lully)

Peter Newble: pp. 19 (decorated bass viol), 62 (shawm), 136 (hpd), 138 (hpd)
Selmer: pp. 50 (cl), 51 (bass cl, sax), 54 (cl), 70 (body manufacture), 71 (bell manufacture), 73 (E flat cl, basset hn, bass cl), 83 (all saxes)
Rolf Tinlin: pp. 48, 49 (mandolin)
Clark Vandergrift: p. 5, 7 (Marin Alsop)
Yamaha pp. 10 (cl) 19 (vn, va), 23 (vn, va), 26 (vn), 30 (va), 68 (cl), 70 (cl keys, reed), 73 (B flat cl, A cl), 80 (sax), 105 (cl), 106 (dbl hn), 111 (euph), 144 (hammers), 145 (upright pf)
Arthur Ka Wai Jenkins / Yamaha: pp. 21 (vn parts), 22 (vn), 24 (vn), 28 (bow), 52 (fl), 53 (ob reed, cl reed), 54 (cl bell), 58 (fl parts), 64 (ob parts), 65 (ob), 67 (ob, ob reed), 69 (cl), 81 (sax), 82 (sax), 88 (mouthpieces), 89 (trbn slide, piston valves, rotary valves), 94 (tpt), 95 (tpt x 4), 96 (tpt bell, B flat tpt, D tpt), 100 (trbn slide, trbn), 101 (hand on slide), 106 (mouthpiece, valves, hn tubing), 110 (mouthpiece), 146 (pedals)

All effort has been made to correctly acknowledge quotations and pictures where appropriate; we apologize for any omissions and would be happy to rectify any such errors if informed.